17359

St. Michae
19292 EI T

P9-EDZ-507

DATE DUE

921
Gue

17359

Solesmes and Dom Gueranger,
1805-1875

DEMCO

SOLESMES AND DOM GUERANGER
1805-1875

Dom Louis Soltner
Translated by Joseph O'Connor

Series Editor, Dr. Richard J. Pugsley

PARACLETE PRESS
Orleans, Massachusetts

Special thanks are due to Mrs. Patricia Buckley Bozell
for her corrections and helpful suggestions
during the preparation of this English language edition.

Copyright © 1995 by Abbaye Saint-Pierre de Solesmes. All rights reserved. This book, or parts thereof, may not be reproduced in any form or by any means except by a newspaper or magazine reviewer who wishes to quote brief passages in connection with a review.

Library of Congress Cataloging-in-Publication Data

Soltner, Louis.
    [Solesmes & Dom Guéranger, 1805-1875. English]
    Solesmes and Dom Guéranger, 1805-1875/Louis Soltner; translated by Joseph O'Connor; foreword by Guy-Marie Oury.
        p.   cm.
    ISBN 1-55725-150-9

    1. Abbaye Saint-Pierre de Solesmes—History—19th century. 2. Guéranger, Prosper, 1806-1875. 3. Abbots—France—Biography. 4. Benedictines—France—Biography.   I. Title.

BX2615.S57S6413   1995
271'.102—dc20
[B]   95-21549
                                                              CIP

10 9 8 7 6 5 4 3 2

Printed in the United States of America at Paraclete Press.

TABLE OF CONTENTS

FOREWORD

DOM GUERANGER DIED AT AGE SEVENTY, a rather short life by today's standards, but a life crowded with events. Born in 1805, one year after the proclamation of the Napoleonic Empire, he died in 1875, while the Third Republic was being consolidated. During his lifetime, he witnessed a long succession of regimes:

—The First Empire, Napoleon Bonaparte (1804 -1814)

—The first Restoration of the Bourbons (June 1814 - March 1815)

—The return of Napoleon and the Hundred Days (March 20 - June 22, 1815)

—The second Restoration of the Bourbons (1815 -1830)

—The July 1830 Revolution

—The July monarchy of Louis-Philippe d'Orleans (1830 - 1848)

—The Revolution of February 1848

—The Second Republic (1848 -1852)

—The Second Empire, Napoleon III (1852 -1870)

—The September 4, 1870, coup and installation of the Third Republic

—The Paris Commune insurrection following the Franco-Prussian War (March-May 1871)

—The provisional Third Republic (with the intention of restoring the monarchy)

The continuing instability signaled a divided society. It was not until 1875 that a slim majority was rounded up to install the Republican regime that was to rule France until the advent of World War II.

The abbot of Solesmes was not very interested in politics; if anything, he probably leaned toward the Napoleonic regime of his youth. But he was deeply concerned with the restoration of the Catholic religion, which, during the French Revolution (1789-1799), along with the destruction of all the structures of the Old Regime, had been ravaged and cut off from its Christian roots.

The French Revolution is said to have started in 1789 and ended in 1799. In fact, it began long before, and the Napoleonic era was in many ways a prolongation and consolidation of the Revolution; during that period, new institutions took shape in lasting laws (the Napoleonic Code).

In 1789, everybody was longing for change, longing to erase the obsolete features that permeated society. The matter of religion split the nation in two, and played a major role in every future event.

In consultation with the parishes of the entire country (*Cahiers de Doléance*) in 1788-1789, a frequent proposal was to allow the state to use the property of the clergy to save the government from bankruptcy. This had been customarily handled in the past by asking the clergy to donate a "free gift." But when Church properties were nationalized (1789-

1791), the clergy lost their independence entirely. Instead, every priest was given a salary by the state, making him no more than a mere civil servant. It was a sure way of eliminating all priests and religious in the nation.

But that was not all. On October 28, 1789, the French Assembly provisionally suspended all religious vows. Shortly thereafter, on February 13, 1790, it abolished all religious orders. The law read: "The legislation no longer recognizes the solemn monastic vows of religious of both sexes. In consequence, it declares that the Orders and Regular Congregations in which such vows are taken are and will be suppressed forever in France, without possibility of revival."

With these words, fourteen centuries of monastic and religious life came to a halt, much as had happened in the England of Henry VIII. All monasteries—and there were many—were shut down: Benedictines, Cistercians, Carthusians, Norbertines, Franciscans, Dominicans, Carmelites. On top of this, the Assembly, without so much as advising the Pope, on July 12, 1790, adopted a civil constitution of the clergy. The main change it dictated was the appointment of bishops and priests. Under the previous arrangement, the Concordat of Bologne (1516), the king presented a list of new bishops to the Pope, and he in turn gave them canonical status. In the new arrangement, the Assembly, or civil electors, of each *"département"*/diocese would elect the bishops who received their canonical status not from the Pope, but from the metropolitan bishop, or the oldest bishop in the province. As for priests, they were to be elected by a caucus of the electors of each "district" (a subdivision of the département), no matter their religious adherence or personal behavior.

Article 19 of title II reads: "The new bishop cannot ask to be confirmed by the Pope, but he will write and notify him, as head of the universal Church, of his appointment in testimony of the unity of faith and communion with him." In short, it nullified the Pope's power of jurisdiction.

Other new constitutional decrees were equally destructive:

—they gave the Assembly jurisdiction over diocesan affairs

—they gave the Assembly power to denounce the Concordat of Bologne (1516), which had been a bilateral contract

—they implicitly gave the Assembly jurisdiction over the Pope

—the new "civil" decrees infringed on religious affairs and intruded in matters beyond their competence

—the civil constitution of the clergy was, in fact, authored by the autocephalus French Church (as opposed to the Roman Catholic Church) which was under the strict control of the state.

Gallicanism, as it was then, was more a state of mind than a set of defining propositions; it claimed that the French Church had the right to administer its own government with minimum interference from the papacy. This prevented the pro-Gallican clergy from spotting the dangers of the new legislation.

But not so the Pope. He and the bishops roundly condemned it. The lower clergy, however, split on the issue; in the end, only a slight majority refused to take the oath to the state, resulting in a schismatic Church. But soon, everything gave way to the official "republican," i.e., pagan, cults that sprang up in 1793—a time of savage persecution and bloodied martyrs.

When religious tolerance was reinstituted in 1795, it only applied to "jurors" (those pledging allegiance to the state);

priests faithful to Rome were still subject to the guillotine. But the new government (the Directory) was nevertheless unable to check the revival of the old faith, and Napoleon Bonaparte, once in power (the Consulate, 1799), negotiated a new Concordat with the Pope (1802) to reinstate religious peace in France. He hoped to effect a national reconciliation by fusing the old France of Catholicism, still the majority, with the new France of the Revolution.

The Pope and negotiations notwithstanding, Napoleon wanted a Church strictly controlled by his government. To this end, he added a whole new set of regulations to the new Concordat in which he reintroduced almost all the measures he had failed to win when dealing with the Pope. He wanted a clergy which would act as part of the government in matters of public morality, but with little if any independence. And he played on the old traditions of Gallicanism, which was still vigorous among the clergy. Thus the Church in France was still weak in many ways—from her lack of independence to her distrust of the papacy.

Nor did the Concordat allude to the restoration of the religious orders. Napoleon was adamantly against them in respect to men. As for women religious, he allowed their existence only if they spent their time in charitable and educational enterprises.

After the fall of Napoleon and the restoration of the Bourbon monarchy, Catholicism was in somewhat better shape, although still under strict control. Anticlericalism was far from dead, particularly among the antimonarchists. Many skeptics, or Voltairians as they were called, looked on the Church as a mere guarantor of order and property rights. She was the bulwark of the social order, the opiate of the lower classes.

But some great thinkers, such as Joseph de Maistre (1753-

1821) and Louis de Bonald (1754-1840), came up with a philosophical justification to join throne and altar, to resurrect Christianity under an absolute monarchy in order to save society. They also proposed instituting a close union between French Catholics and the Pope, the core of the Church.

The movement spread. De Maistre and de Bonald were laymen, yet Félicité de Lamennais (1782-1854) was a priest, and he became the most powerful voice among the younger clergy to advocate greater independence of the Church from the civil power and a closer union with Rome.

But when the Revolution of 1830 overthrew King Louis Philippe, Lamennais became more extreme in his demands: he now advocated the radical separation of Church and state in order to ensure more freedom for the Church, and to this end launched the newspaper *l'Avenir*, which took radical and violent positions. This led him to a series of clashes with the French bishops, and he appealed to Rome. Forced to take sides, Pope Gregory XVI rebuked him mildly, but then more forcefully when Lamennais refused to renounce his ideas. Eventually Lamennais left the Church, but his disciples remained faithful to the Pope and to Lamennais's original ideal of restoring Catholicism in France.

Restoration of some religious orders finally began under the Bourbon regime of King Louis Philippe 1815-1830; Trappists, Franciscans, and Jesuits reappeared, but their path was far from smooth, as the government swung from toleration to mild persecution.

New apostolic congregations were also founded. Under the restored monarchial regime, largely under the control of a skeptic bourgeoisie, the religious revival began to flourish. The Society of the Propagation of the Faith founded in Lyon by Blessed Pauline Jaricot in 1822 to help the Catholic missions, could boast 700,000 members by 1834; Frédéric

Ozanam's Society of Saint Vincent de Paul, founded in 1833 to visit and care for the poor, quite rapidly opened a hundred branches in the provinces. Women's congregations grew in membership from 25,000 in 1829 to 60,000 in 1844. The secular clergy swelled its ranks to 40,000 members. The sermons of Lacordaire in Notre-Dame in Paris during Lent of 1835 were said to have drawn six thousand men, mostly young intellectuals. The Catholic press expanded, and the newspaper *L'Univers* under Louis Veuillot became one of the most widely read and influential papers in France. Moreover, Gallicanism lost ground among the clergy when a new generation of bishops from a more common background—some of whom had been disciples of Lamennais—took over.

After 1830, except for a very short period, the aristocracy never again played a major role in the political or social life of France. The bourgeoisie took over. From banker and industrialist, to artisan and petty employee of the state, they became proud members of the National Guard, which helped unseat the monarchy in the revolutions of 1830 and 1848.

Urban workers, whose condition had steadily deteriorated, began to plague the Orleans monarchy through industrial upheaval and strikes, which led to the Second Republic in 1848. The unrest in Paris and in some towns in the provinces, led to a coalition whose major elements came from the bourgeois and peasant classes. Thus, when Louis-Napoleon Bonaparte came upon the political scene, he received powerful Catholic backing. His support came from the workers who believed in his concern for their welfare.

Recent studies have established that Napoleon III was a far-sighted technocrat and social reformer, surrounded by a team of former Saint-Simon-type socialists. But neither state socialism nor general prosperity would be able to preserve workers faithful to Bonapartism. The republican opposition became more and more effective, and Napoleon III became the victim of an ongoing smear campaign.

During the Second Republic, the Falloux law of 1850 had been passed; it allowed the Church to expand her efforts to educate the elite and to have a share in running the universities. When the Empire was restored in 1852, it too, especially in its early days, was favorable to the Church. By 1870, religious schools had almost as many pupils as the state secondary schools, which had formerly monopolized education.

But while the influence of Catholicism on society grew steadily until 1870, the opposition from republicans, certain working class movements, and the intelligentsia hardened: they combined in a hard anticlericalism. Starting in 1860, the press, the Freemasons, the Protestant elite, and labor leaders began to make war in earnest against the Church and her institutions.

Catholics, in the meantime, were also concerned about the Italian policy of Napoleon III. Cavour's annexation of papal territory in 1860 had the secret approval of the emperor, outraging Catholics who saw it as gravely dangerous to the independence of the papacy. In response to Catholic criticism, the emperor placed restrictions on the religious press, religious education, and unauthorized religious orders. But the military disaster consequent to the Franco-Prussian War of 1870 led to the deposition of the emperor and the proclamation of the Third Republic by a handful of politicians.

After the armistice, the National Assembly, elected in 1871, turned out to be the most Catholic-oriented since the fall of the Old Regime in 1789. In March of 1871, the Commune of Paris—wildly anticlerical—rose up in a savage effort to seize power, during which Archbishop Darboy of Paris, as well as twenty priests and nuns, were executed.

But soon the Third Republic was again in control. Founded upon a humiliating military defeat, however, the new regime was considered to be provisional, the least offensive, to conservative politicians, of several choices. The politicians were themselves deeply divided over the nature of the monarchy for which they longed.

The system they had—a system of government associated with Jacobin radicalism and bloody deeds perpetrated during the Revolution in the name of the Republic—shocked them deeply. The Third Republic, however, became popular with the peasant electors of the center and south of France, and thus retained power.

* * *

Solesmes is located at the very edge of the province of Maine, near the Anjou border, less than 150 miles southwest of Paris. The village grew around an old Benedictine priory founded in the beginning of the eleventh century by the monks of Saint-Pierre de la Couture Abbey in Le Mans. Rebuilt and restored several times—after the Hundred Years' War, the Religious Wars of the sixteenth century, and so on—it was finally closed in 1790 by the revolutionaries, one of the two hundred Benedictine houses whose 2,500 monks were dispersed throughout the country.

More fortunate than many of the other monasteries, the Priory of Solesmes was kept largely intact by those who bought it when it was sold by the state. Standing next to the river Sarthe, not far from the little town of Sablé, this monastery, with its eighteenth-century white buildings and its ancient eleventh-century church (restored in the late fifteenth and early sixteenth centuries) houses some of the most beautiful statues of the pre- and late-Renaissance.

Prosper Guéranger was born in Sablé and was familiar from his earliest years with the dilapidated priory. As a child, visiting the ruins, he dreamed of becoming a hermit, living in the nearby caves of La Hartempied.

Today, the Solesmes congregation is made up of thirty monasteries of monks and nuns in Europe, Africa, the Caribbean, and North America (Canada and Vermont). The spirit of Dom Guéranger had a strong influence on some of the other Benedictine congregations and monasteries, especially in Germany, Belgium, England, Brazil, and Argentina.

But it is time to start the account of his life.

Fr. Guy-Marie Oury

I

CHILDHOOD
AND YOUTH

"SABLE, MY HOMELAND. . . " When Dom Guéranger wrote these words in a letter to his friend Charles Louvet, he expressed more than his civilian status: he proclaimed that he was a true native of the soil.

An official report from 1802 spoke of the inhabitants of Sablé as being "of good blood, agile in appearance, good society," and added that "their liveliness and pleasant conversation were the effects of living near the Maine-et-Loire region." Perhaps Prosper Guéranger did benefit from these good geographical influences. But to the best of our knowledge his ancestry does not trace back to Anjou (the region around Angers, immediately to the west of Sablé, between the "Maine and Loire" rivers). Rather, his family reaches back to the area around Le Mans (the town approximately 25 miles east of Sablé).

Dom Guéranger's father, Pierre, was born in Le Mans in 1773, son of Julien Guéranger, a muslin manufacturer who set up shop in the Gourdaine parish, and of Marie Davoust, originally from Pontlieue. At the outbreak of the French Revolution in 1789, Pierre, who was considering taking Holy Orders, was forcibly enrolled in the army of the Republic, but soon managed to get free and return home.

In 1797, he appears again in Sainte-Suzanne, located in La Mayenne, where he had probably been drawn by relatives who lived there. And it was there that on January 27, 1798, he married Françoise Jary, a seamstress born in the neighboring town of Saint-Jean-sur-Erve. Françoise was the daughter of Victor Jary, a master cobbler, and Anne Chapon.

During those years, Catholic priests who had refused to take the revolutionary oath out of fidelity to Rome still lived in fear. The marriage was therefore blessed in secret by Father Michel Barrabé, who had returned from exile in the Isle of Jersey only the year before, and who resided in the parish of Chammes, not far from Sainte-Suzanne. This wooded region of Le Maine, called "la Charnie," was somewhat divided politically.

The "Chouans," or antirevolutionary and active royalists, controlled the countryside, but the city dwellers were longing for peace, which was indispensible to small industries and commerce. Napoleon, with his newly founded Empire, seemed to hold out a sure promise of this tranquility, and the Concordat that he concluded with Rome in 1802 guaranteed freedom of religious worship.

These factors help explain why the Guérangers, with their profound religious faith and their loyalty to France, so easily rallied round the new regime. And they supported it to the very end, even though they deplored Napoleon's persecution of Pope Pius VII. In much the same manner, in 1815, common sense and a complete lack of political prejudice, along with their desire for peace, brought them to accept the Restoration of the Bourbon monarchy with no difficulty.

This open and straightforward attitude, which kept the Catholic faith alive and sheltered it from the endemic political passions, deserves mention. For it was a policy that Dom Guéranger himself would adopt and never abandon throughout the entire period of the frequent political upheavals through which he lived.

Shortly after his marriage, and for reasons unknown, Pierre Guéranger settled down in Sablé. Perhaps he had some distant relative there also. In any case, because of his liking and aptitude for teaching, he opened a school in what had once been the convent of the Cordelier (Franciscan) Sisters of Saint-Elisabeth, founded in the seventeenth century. This establishment was located at the entry to a suburb called Saint-Nicolas. And it was here that Pierre's four sons were born, Frédéric, Edouard, Prosper, and Constantin.

Few traces remain of the home in which Dom Guéranger was born. Since then, the former convent-buildings of the Fransiscan sisters have undergone many transformations, and today only one vestige going back to the time of Dom Guéranger's birth is still visible: an ancient stairway leading to a magnificent framewood attic.

In 1808, the Guérangers exchanged this dwelling for the one occupied by the gendarmes on the nearby islet on the River Sablé, within feet of the church of Notre-Dame. This building had originally been a boarding school, established in 1602 to house thirty students. Curiously enough, in the distant past, it had belonged to the monks of the ancient priory of Solesmes.

Prosper-Louis-Pascal was baptised on the very evening of the day of his birth, April 4, 1805. The ceremony took place in the old parish church, Notre-Dame, which has now disappeared, but its baptismal font has been transferred to the new church of the same name. The name "Prosper" was uncommon in the region. Like the names of his other sons, it indicates a somewhat studied choice on the part of Pierre Guéranger. That year, April 4 fell on the Thursday before Palm Sunday, and hence the middle name "Pascal." "Louis" was probably chosen in honor of the child's godfather, Father Louis Gazeau, a priest-friend of the family, who had spent time in prison at Laval in 1792.

Almost nothing would have been known about Prosper Guéranger's childhood and youth if he himself had not written his own *Memoires*, in order to prevent the spread of legends about himself. This autobiography, which unfortunately only goes as far as the year 1833, is very interesting and full of zest.

The child Prosper grew up in a Sablé that existed then, and can be seen in ancient engravings: an extremely picturesque town with its eighteenth-century château, its frequent river traffic, which is hard for us to imagine today, and its population of three thousand inhabitants. These were made up largely of tradespeople and craftsmen, who were well known for their marbleworks and glovemaking.

Dom Guéranger was always very discreet about his family environment. He saved none of his parents' letters, for example. Nevertheless, a glimpse of Pierre Guéranger's somewhat austere figure comes out; from the time he first thought of entering the priesthood, he began to recite the Hours, and the parish registries give evidence of his commitment to the clergy of Sablé.

Though no physical description of her exists, Madame Jary was, it seems, small and active with a spirited humor that compensated for her husband's gravity. To her, Prosper owed his liveliness and playfulness, while from his father he inherited the tranquil strength that appears in all his work.

The contrast is apparent from his very first years: he was

given to lively repartee, an intense curiosity, and wild games inspired by the military trappings of the imperial epoch; but he also indulged in childish imitations of the ceremonies of the Church, and was given to meditative strolls to the deserted priory of Solesmes, two miles distant. The family servant, a native of the little town, brought him there at an early age. Already eight centuries old, the monastery, founded in 1010 by Geoffroy de Sablé, seemed quite dead. The last prior, expelled from his monastery in 1791 and subsequently imprisoned for his faith, had died near Le Mans several years earlier. Prosper had undoubtedly heard tell about another monk of Solesmes, Dom Papion, who, after his detention, had come back to exercise his ministry at Sablé, where he died of old age in 1819.

The child must many a time have been lost in wonder as he stood before the mysterious statues of the monastery, dreaming dreams, and later the young man must often have meditated as he walked alone on the rocks of La Poulie, yet there was never any presentiment of a monastic future. Dom Guéranger took pains to point this out to keep any romantic legends from springing up. The only firm fact was his attachment to the site and to the old Benedictine monastery.

Learning to read was a game for him, and soon reading became his favorite recreation. The speed and scope of his reading were generally admired, but, in truth, his enthusiasm ought to have been moderated; it did no harm to read Fénelon or Chateaubriand the whole day long in the woods or in the niche of some rock, but the same did not hold true of his poring over books in his seminary room or in murky libraries.

Still, his love of books did not make the child lose sight of the deep religious questions of his time. His family formation saw to this. Pierre Guéranger, whose school was described as "the fruits of fanaticism" by a report of the superintendent of police, taught his sons never to be afraid to affirm their faith. Every evening, he read them the life of the saint of the day. The courage of older times, moreover, lived on in him when he gave hospitality to priests who dared confess the faith during the Revolution.

In these ways he created an atmosphere of heroic fidelity, and his children accepted the years of persecution endured for the freedom of the Church. The entire family prayed for the Pope. The boy Prosper remembered how impressed he was by an engraving that pictured Pius VII at the feet of Our Lady of Sorrows. From both discretion and shame, the Pope's captivity at Fontainbleau was hidden from him, until he learned of it by chance when he was about seven years old. He was totally distraught, but all unconsciously, it reinforced his attachment to the Church and to its leader.

The voice of God had found an echo in this young and fruitful soul, in this precocious child—and it spoke of a vocation to the priesthood. After his first studies at Sablé, his First Holy Communion in 1816, and his Confirmation the following year, given by Bishop Charles Montault at Morannes, he was sent in 1818 as a scholarship student to the Collège Royal in Angers.

As his father had already started him on Latin, he entered the fourth form and pursued his studies up to the completion of rhetoric in 1822. Though not head of the class, he was a good student and was able to indulge in such pastimes as poetry and, of course, reading.

"He had a style about him, a rare thing among collegians," wrote one of his fellow students. "Born with a serious character and an intellect above his age, he did not join much in the games of his comrades. He preferred walking to chatting. His conversation was sometimes playful, more often serious, and always instructive. We were happy to listen to him, and he always gave good counsel." In fact, he formed lasting friendships at Angers, notably with Charles Louvet, future mayor of Saumur and minister of the Second Empire; in later years, he helped Louvet recover his faith.

The students of Angers were no altar boys. Because Prosper impressed them with his piety—communing at each of the four great feastdays—they nicknamed him "monk," which he put up with quite cheerfully.

Given his predilection for reading, it was hardly surprising that the adolescent threw himself into the works of the great authors of the time—the *Génie du christianisme*, the *Martyrs*, and so on. *Les Méditations* of Lamartine made him wish to read the Bible, while Bossuet and Fleury assuaged his taste for history. Nearly all the great French and foreign literature passed through his hands, thanks to the help of a young chaplain of the college, the abbé Pasquier.

His particular favorites, however, were two contemporary writers who were interested in the religious problems of the epoch: Joseph de Maistre and Félicité de Lamennais. The *Soirées de Saint-Petersbourg*, the *Considérations sur la France*, and above all *Le Pape*, which he read pencil in hand, gave him a glimpse of the role of the Pope in history. In de Maistre, whom he held was "the greatest genius of recent times," Dom Guéranger found not only a simple and firm style, but profound views on the antinomy between the authority of God and the authority (entrusted by God to the ruling power) of government. After reading him, he realized that, despite appearances, under the Restoration, the spirit that inspired the French Revolution was just as virulent and more dangerous than ever. In addition, he was struck by de Maistre's historical demonstration of papal sovereignty throughout the centuries, as well as his speculations on the natural infallibility of all sovereign authority.

In a similar manner, Guéranger absorbed Lamennais's renowned *Essai sur l'indifférence,* in which he set out to prove that society could not regain stability unless it were founded on the religious authority of Church and Pope. Although Prosper Guéranger assimilated it, he only partially understood the philosophical considerations on "common sense" that were a reaction against the rationalism of the previous century.

As for the politics of the day, the college student was not too moved, except on the occasion of the Duc de Berry's assassination in 1820, which roused some royalist feelings in him, but they were only temporary.

At the beginning of 1821, the Guérangers left Sablé for Le Mans. The school in Sablé had begun to receive serious competition from the Minor Seminary of Précigné, and after twenty-three years of teaching, Pierre Guéranger wanted a better and more restful post in the city of his ancestors. He taught a fifth form class at the Collège Royal, until around 1838, when he retired to the rue Saint-Vincent, where he died ten years later.

Prosper, whose vocation never wavered, entered the Seminary of Le Mans and, in 1822, was clothed in the cassock along with seventy other students, of whom forty would persevere to the priesthood. At that time, the year of philosophy was taught in the old Hôtel Tesse, which dominated the Promenade des Jacobins, not far from the apse of the cathedral, while the theology students were located at the Séminaire Saint-Vincent.

This new period of Dom Guéranger's life was devoted to his intellectual and spiritual formation. The mediocrity of his ecclesiastical studies was offset by his reading and perceptive insights, which enlightened his research. In his autobiography, Dom Guéranger severely criticizes these clerical studies, hardly surprising given the *Institutiones philosophicae* of Lyon and the *Institutiones theologicae* of Poitiers. There was, he fulminates, "absolutely no course in ecclesiastical history, liturgy, or canon law, absolutely no mystic or ascetic theology, and, in the seminary, very little godliness." St. Thomas, Suarez, and many other greats were simply ignored.

The examinations of conscience of Tronson, and the spiritual conferences of Abbé Bouvier, future bishop of Le Mans, left his soul undernourished, suffering from method and minutiae and an intense dryness. His spirit needed a wider range of thought.

More at ease with literary disciplines than with the exact sciences, the young Prosper at first feared he would never be able to assimilate logic. Latin was a further difficulty. But when his old chaplain from Angers pointed out to him how well-constructed arguments could help religion, he overcame his aversion. One of the most remarkable qualities of his future works would be precisely the rigorous strength of reasoning; given the author's bent of mind, it would be used in historical documents more than in strict philosophic constructions.

Because of the pervasive undisciplined atmosphere, of which the professors seemed unaware, Prosper sat near the lecture chair with several other serious students in order to follow the courses. He drew little attention to himself, and was largely unnoticed as a student.

On August 10, 1823, in the chapel of the Visitation, he received the tonsure, and in that moment felt himself definitely consecrated to God. One year later, on the same day and in the same church, he received the four minor orders.

Vacations permitted him to plunge into his element; the seminary library was open to him. He was in rapture. "This is when I began to know books. I experienced an unparalleled happiness when I finally studied them in-folio. These publications of the Fathers of the Church ravished me; never had I fingered through them . . . the historians, the hagiographers, and above all the Society of the Bollandists. It all left a profound impression on me; I felt I was living a much more intense life, for I now knew exactly what these books were."

The enchantment implanted in him a desire for the Benedictine life. The beautiful folios of the Maurists fascinated the young cleric, who yearned to study the sources of the ecclesiastical sciences. He liked to imagine going to Monte Cassino (the possibility of a Benedictine restoration in France had not even flickered in his mind). These thoughts consumed him right up to his ordination, but they then vanished. They were, it seemed, nothing but a passing fancy, born of a misconception of monasticism. He was, in fact, quite unaware of the fundamentals of the religious life. Nevertheless, the thought had been seeded, and in 1831 it would reawaken and mature.

His "tranquil rage" for books during the summer of 1824—a book, of whatever sort, a day—became a serious health hazard and, indeed, he fell sick. The academic year was lost, but it was recaptured the next summer because, once back on his feet, he began a methodic and more reflective reading of the Apostolic Fathers, which he pursued during his third and last year of seminary. The archives of Solesmes conserve the huge binder of notes he took during this personal study—the first fruits of his assiduous reading of the Church Fathers, and one of his enduring strengths. "I vowed that for my entire life," Dom Guéranger wrote, "I would devote myself to ecclesiastical antiquity." He did not exaggerate.

The spiritual life of Prosper Guéranger, not hitherto known for its great fervor, was graced right from the start of his seminary years. But the most notable event took place on the morning of December 8, 1823—"the grace of the Immaculate Conception," as it came to be known. Up until then, he had harbored some rationalist prejudices concerning this mystery, which the Church had not yet defined as dogma. He had not, that is, understood its relationship to the mystery of the Incarnation. Suddenly, during his meditation on the theme of the feast of that day, his reason joined his heart in total belief. "No transport whatsoever, but a sweet peace with a sincere conviction. . . It was one nature disappearing to make way for another."

One result is certain: it hastened his theological synthesis, found in his first writings, which are centered on the mystery of the Incarnation.

In another area, the ideas of Lamennais continued to stimulate him. In his rhetoric classes he had, from the start, declared himself "squarely Lamennaisian," but he had not properly understood the terms of the great debate which divided the clergy and, even more, the professors of the seminary. A seminarian can, of course, be excused for distinguishing imperfectly between the natural and the supernatural orders when his studies don't even include a treatise on Faith. But Prosper Guéranger later escaped unscathed from the philosophical discussions on "common sense," which contended that individual reason did not have the capacity to come to truth, and which Rome, incidentally, condemned in 1834—thanks to his faith, to his fidelity to the magisterium, and to his theological depth, not to mention his defiance of philosophy as taught at the time.

"But another long-lasting and more salutary crisis," he reports in his autobiography, "then took place in the Church of France. Gallicanism received the most terrible blows. Lamennais tore it limb from limb, and the whole of the younger, more studious clergy hastened to follow such an athlete." Forty years later, as can be seen, Dom Guéranger was still shaken at the memory.

Joseph de Maistre was too far above the intellectual level of most clerics to make much of an impression. Lamennais, on the other hand, through his hard and passionate eloquence, was able to transmit to others the Roman ideal—that all Catholics unite around the Head of the Church.

His book, *On Religion in its Connection with Political and Civil Order*, attacked the Gallican Church's famous Declaration of Four Articles of 1682, which were condemned by two popes, and could have led to an Anglican-type schism by minimizing control by Rome. Lamennais was disavowed by fourteen bishops and strongly opposed by many others, which only deepened the chasm between the old clergy and the new, the backers of the Concordat.

The monthly *Mémorial catholique*, put out by Abbé Olympe-Philippe Gerbet and Abbé Louis-Antoine de Salinis, kept this "generation to whom belongs the awakening of France," in the words of Dom Guéranger, aroused. The profusion and clarity of articles in the review helped the seminarian judge the past as well as the events of his own time, and helped rid him of the last prejudices inherited from Gallicanism. In the doing, he revised his position in regards the papacy. The change was decisive; the nuances would come later.

At twenty-one years of age, Prosper Guéranger ended his three years of theological study. Still too young to be ordained, he had to take up a temporary position and wait. For a short while, he was upset at leaving his beloved patristic studies behind. But his spirits lightened when, instead of a professorship at Château-Gontier, he was offered the position of secretary to the bishop.

Mgr. Claude-Madeleine de la Myre-Mory, who had governed the diocese of Le Mans since 1819, had recently become paralyzed. This seventy-year-old prelate, a dignified man of the world and a representative of the episcopate during the last days of the *Ancien Régime,* spent the revolutionary period in Italy and Austria before reentering France to accept, in a moment of weakness, the post of vicar general to Cardinal Maury in 1810.

In this man's service, Prosper Guéranger would begin a brief but important phase of his formation, making many contacts that would serve him well in the future. The old bishop, moreover, took a liking to his young companion, whom he found alert and observant, and the youth benefited from the older man's long experience of men and events.

II

SECULAR PRIEST

IN JULY 1826, PROSPER GUERANGER WAS ORDAINED subdeacon
and began reciting the breviary with joy and pride. It was not
the traditional Roman breviary, but the new French version
promulgated in 1748 by Mgr. Charles-Louis de Froullay,
bishop of Le Mans—a version that lacked the distinguishing
touch of the Fathers.

On November 21, the new deacon gave his first sermon at
the Dames du Sacré-Cœur; he was chagrined when his
memory failed and he had to delve into his pockets to retrieve
his notes. After repeated failures of memory, he gave up
trying to learn his sermon by heart and instead jotted down
several ideas which he would then develop spontaneously. In
future years, he became known, not for his grandiloquence,
but for his direct and simple style. His clarity, but most of all
his enthusiasm won over his listeners.

During this time, Guéranger was secretary to
Monseigneur de la Myre. When in the spring of 1827, the
monseigneur left to take the waters at Borbonne, Guéranger

traveled to Angers to receive the diaconate from Mgr. Charles Montault. After Easter, he returned to Le Mans to prepare for the great day of his priestly ordination; because of his youth, his bishop had had to obtain a dispensation of eighteen months.

On October 7, 1827, Prosper Guéranger was ordained a priest by Mgr. Charles de Montblanc in the oratory of the archbishop's palace at Tours with no liturgical solemnity whatsoever. In fact, as he later recounted, during the ceremony, he realized that the bishop had entirely forgotten to lay hands on him, and Guéranger had to nudge his memory.

That afternoon, Abbé Guéranger made a solitary pilgrimage to the ruins of the Abbey of Marmoutiers, founded in 371, where he underwent still another emotional experience. Kneeling before the altar of St. Martin, the young priest, reciting the *Rorate,* was flooded with thoughts from his seminary days about the splendor of monastic life. Pondering on the present desolation of the Church, he thought his heart would break. On leaving the chapel, he encountered an elderly woman, and his pain intensified as she depicted the acts of vandalism she had witnessed in her lifetime, the ringing hammer blows that smashed the choir windows into flying bursts of stained glass, and other depredations. Saddened, he went his way.

Two days later, with his family in attendance, Abbé Guéranger celebrated his first Mass in the Lady Chapel in the apse of the cathedral of Le Mans, and he was gripped by fresh fervor.

From the very day of Abbé Guéranger's ordination, the bishop had decided to appoint him to the rank of canon at the cathedral. This provoked a small outburst of jealousy from various members of the chapter: the newcomer was only twenty-two years old! (This would not be the last time the young man would cause problems for the bishop.)

The 1828 feast of Saint Julien, patron of the diocese of Le Mans, was a high point in the life of the future abbot of Solesmes: on that day he obtained permission to pray in unison with the Roman Church. Now, through Rome's liturgical books, he could "enter ever more deeply into the inmost consciousness of the Church." In allowing him to use the Roman missal and breviary, Monseigneur de la Myre gave him a treasure not generally obtainable in the diocese of Le Mans. Two years later, the gift bore fruit: from his daily immersion in the Church's prayer, Dom Guéranger was inspired to write papers that were the determinative influence in reestablishing liturgical unity in France.

In May 1828, Monseigneur de la Myre left Le Mans for Paris, and a few months later, due to ill health, sent his resignation to Rome. His secretary, Dom Guéranger, followed him during his last difficult years. For the first time in his life, he was outside his province, separated from his own, and it affected him deeply. But his travels enlarged his horizons; they gave him a glimpse of the varied aspects of the nation and the opportunity to meet other members of the French clergy. Given his spiritual alertness, he was bound to glean great good from this practical experience. He discovered the beauty of Chartres and the vivacity of Paris—which he never really liked—and he admired the fidelity to Rome of the Franche Comté clergy, among whom he made various friends: the future Cardinal Thomas Gousset, the future Mgr. Ferdinand Donnet, and others. And he shivered with cold at Bourbonne, where he became "chaplain of the bathers."

At Marolle, a little town on the Seine-et-Oise that had no priest, he undertook to revitalize the faith and was so successful that those poor people asked him to remain as their pastor. And everywhere, it seemed, he brushed up against the evil of de-Christianization, which was difficult for someone from Le Mans to comprehend.

In Paris, Monseigneur de la Myre usually resided at the Séminaire des Mission Etrangères, rue du Bac, where he received socially prominent visitors. As his secretary, Dom Guéranger took over the appointment calendar, but he did not know that he was hobnobbing with members of the secret society of the Chevaliers de la Foi, a sort of Catholic Freemasonry; the family of the bishop of Le Mans was in fact connected to the family of Count Ferdinand de Bertier, the society's founder. Abbé Guéranger watched and listened as these aristocrats who had survived the Revolution reminisced about the grandeurs of yesteryear. As he reflected on the strengths and weaknesses of that society, he came to realize that despite its charm, it could never reestablish Christianity in France. The Revolution was past, but the Restoration had "neither forgotten anything nor learned anything."

From this aristocratic milieu, the young secretary acquired a layer of urbanity which was needed to counter a certain brusqueness and overfamiliarity in him. He also had the pleasure of running into Dom Antoine Saulnier de Beauregard, the famous abbé of Melleray, whom he had met at the bishop's palace in Le Mans and who, coincidentally, had attended his ordination. Dom Guéranger remembered him vividly: "I have never had a more enjoyable or keen experience than in conversing with Dom Antoine. Along with a perfect decorum, he had a sparkling wit, overlaid with the aura of the *Ancien Régime*, which made his nobility felt a mile away, and he was in perfect possession of what was then called the tone of the old court; my bishop, much a man of the world, paled next to him, although he came across as a true monk in every respect. He was admired at court and in the town houses of the old French aristocracy, and every year, a trip to Paris was de rigueur. He accepted me as his friend, and told the bishop that he wished me to go to Melleray. The bishop warned me of this, but there was little danger: I felt no attraction for the Trappist life, which would have meant the end of my studies."

The numerous letters to his brother Edouard, as well as his autobiography, are the best sources of Abbé Guéranger's thoughts during his years in Paris. There, he closely followed the political events and their repercussions on the clergy; he felt that the cause of the Bourbons was steadily deteriorating, that it was hopeless, in fact.

One voice seemed to agree with him; it warned of the perils of the times, but it also indicated how Catholicism and society could be renewed. It was early in 1829, and Lamennais had just published his book, *On the Progress of the Revolution and the War against the Church*. As soon as he had read it, Dom Guéranger wrote the author to congratulate him and sent him a project he had been working on: a compilation of proof of the sovereignty of the Pope gleaned from Tradition—a sort of historic-dogmatic treatise. He hoped to refute the current prejudices against the papacy through facts.

From his home in la Chênaie, near Saint Malo in Brittany, Lamennais responded with encouragement, bibliographical references for his studies, and a pressing invitation to join the little group of ecclesiastics that revolved around him to help him bring about "the regeneration of society." As he was still acting as secretary to Monseigneur de la Myre, Dom Guéranger replied that he was not free, but that he hoped with all his heart for the success of their work.

Was Dom Guéranger to be taken literally? In a sense, yes. He was quite sincere in calling Lamennais *"maître,"* in looking upon him as providential to the renovation of France, and in declaring his devotion to his doctrines—but he never ceded his independence. There was actually no real friendship between the two men; the relationship was more accurately admiration on the part of the disciple and benevolent interest on that of the master. Their correspondence, which ended in December 1832, bears this out, as does the direction Dom Guéranger took after the death of Monseigneur de la Myre freed him from his duties.

The elderly prelate died on September 8, 1829, at the Château du Gué-à-Trême, in the diocese of Meaux. Before his death, thanks to Dom Guéranger's promptings, he renounced the Gallican maxims in favor of the traditional Roman doctrines. Abbé Guéranger immediately sent the official record of Myre's profession of faith to the chapter at Le Mans.

Now free, Dom Guéranger considered going to la Chênaie to work with Lamennais. He discussed the possibility with Abbé Olympe Gerbet, the most eminent disciple of Lamennais, but in the end, due to lack of funds and his diocesan situation—he belonged to the clergy of Le Mans—he decided to continue to live in Paris. He obtained a post at the parish of the Missions Etrangères, which allowed him time for his studies and to enjoy the great libraries. But despite all this, he yearned for his province of le Maine. Characteristically, Dom Guéranger felt uneasy when far from his family. (Later on he had similar difficulties living apart from his monks.) His mother died on June 15, 1829, after a long illness, and he was broken-hearted not to have been present, even at the services, despite his efforts.

The advantageous offers he had received through the de la Myre family, such as entree to the Grande Aumônerie, had not interested him. He didn't want to tie his future to an unsettled dynasty. Besides, the modus vivendi among the pastor of the Missions Etrangères, the abbé Desgenettes, and himself, the assistant pastor, was quite satisfactory: "My pastor knows that I want to study, and helps as much as possible by giving me the means."

The ministry, in fact, amounted to very little; because of his youthful looks, he was assigned to teach catechism and preach sermons rather than hear confessions. Among the occasional ceremonies over which he presided was the annual pilgrimage to the great calvary of Mont-Valérien. During one of them, which Dom Guéranger has described picturesquely, the old King Charles X sang the *Domine, salvum fac regem* (Lord, save the king) with all his heart less than two months before his fall in July 1830.

If the assistant pastor had really had a vocation to an active apostolate, it would surely have manifested itself at Marolles or Paris. But, on the contrary, as he recalled to his brother, though he applied himself conscientiously, he felt absolutely no attraction to the ministry. He wanted to serve the Church through his studies.

Some years before, on the advice of Monseigneur de la Myre, he had chosen as his director of conscience a famous Jesuit, Père Joseph Varin, who helped him comprehend the spiritual life. "Without having a really clear picture of it, I began to feel what it was to be a religious." The maturity of judgment that is evident in Dom Guéranger's very first letters of spiritual direction no doubt stems from this early formation.

"One single goal motivated all my efforts: the defense of Rome," he wrote. While Dom Guéranger was waiting for the results of the first fruits of his activity in this field, Lamennais encouraged him to write several articles for the *Mémorial Catholique.* This suggestion came at a propitious moment for Abbé Guéranger; had he not paused to write, his knowledge would have remained mere erudition—inactive, sterile.

"My intellect," he wrote, "was waiting for a signal to get

underway and to do something productive with the attraction that I felt for erudition. This signal was in fact given me by the liturgy, although I was unaware of it at the time. The school of M. de Lamennais was looking above all for general ideas; I perceived the dogma of the Incarnation as the center to which I had to bring everything back; the dogma of the Church is enclosed in that of the Incarnation. The sacraments, the sacramentals, the poetry of the prayers and liturgical actions, all of that appeared more and more radiant to me. I felt that the future of my mind was in these areas."

At age twenty-five, he already had a remarkably unified train of thought. The four articles he published from February to July of 1830 under the title *Thoughts on the Catholic Liturgy* contained all the ideas he would later develop. In these pages, he attacked the strong Gallican and Jansenist positions, and argued that because the liturgy is the language of the Church, it must be ancient, universal, authorized, and godly. His writing demonstrates the foresight and cogency of his intuitions—and of his youth (as he would later acknowledge): the polemic that followed the *Ami de la religion et du roi* (Friend of Religion and the King), one of the four, was barely courteous. More important, the controversy was a warning to Dom Guéranger that he would have to renounce his own peace and quiet if he wished to dislodge Gallicanism from its entrenched position in France.

This same youthful and appealing enthusiasm led to his decision, and that of Abbé Desgenettes, to consecrate Sunday, July 4, 1830, to the Roman cause. Since the octave of Saint Peter was being celebrated that same day, the parishioners sat through two long sermons, one on the rights of the Pope, the other against the Four Articles of 1682. Dom Guéranger then left to take his vacation in Le Mans.

While he was there, the summer calm was shattered by

the outbreak of the July Revolution. This 1830 revolution replaced the legitimate Bourbon with Louis-Philippe's bourgeois regime.

Among other things, the revolution's violent anticlericalism forced priests to don lay clothes for protection. Dom Guéranger recounted how, thanks to this disguise, he was able to return to his post at Les Missions. He also told how he tricked an insurgent into letting him attend to his (the insurgent's) mother who had asked for the last rites.

M. Desgenettes, who had fled to Switzerland, invited his former assistant to join him there to run a newspaper. Dom Guéranger would have preferred to collaborate on the newspaper *L'Avenir*, which had recently replaced the *Mémorial Catholique*, as Lamennaise advised, but in the end, he decided instead to go back to Le Mans. He had obtained the permission of Mgr. Philippe-Marie Guy Carron, the new bishop, to pursue his work there while undertaking a part-time ministry. As fall approached, the priest left his Parisian life with few regrets.

At Le Mans, although he missed the libraries, he enjoyed the same tranquil and studious life he had had in Paris, as well as the charming surroundings of le Maine. The fortunate young honorary canon could devote himself entirely to his personal work, and with no scruples, for he willingly took on whatever tasks were asked of him. As always, because of his youthful air, he was called less to the confessional than to the pulpit, preaching sermons at the cathedral for the chapter, in the parishes of the city, or at the private boarding school of Sacré-Cœur. He soon acquired the reputation of being "ready [to preach] on whatever the subject." When he spoke from the fullness of his heart, moreover, he lost the slight speech impediment that ordinarily kept him from achieving real eloquence.

What, in the meantime, had become of his vast work on the papacy? The exigencies of the moment had relegated it to the background. His tendency of allowing great undertakings to wait upon an immediate concern was already evident. This trait, about which he was often reproached, stemmed from his ardent temperament, his love of variety, and, above all, from his total devotion to the Church, which demanded resolution to an immediate problem or threat.

Invited to collaborate on the new publication of the Lamennaisian school, Abbé Guéranger published two articles entitled *On Prayer for the King* in *L'Avenir* in late October. In these articles, he attempted to overcome the reluctance of Catholic legitimists to say the *Domine, salvum fac regem* for the usurper, Louis-Philippe. While demonstrating that the Church has always prayed for governments, inasmuch as they are responsible for civil order, Abbé Guéranger emphasized the right of the Church to total freedom from temporal power.

In like manner, he examined a grave problem brought back to prominence by the change of government in France: the selection of bishops by a heretical or agnostic prince, e.g., Napoleon, Louis XVIII, or Louis Philippe. The Concordat had envisioned just such a case, and it was an opportune time to recall its principles now that the Catholic religion was no longer recognized as, in Anglican terminology, "the Established Church."

Taking up the Church's case, Dom Guéranger drafted *On the Election and Nomination of Bishops,* which appeared in June 1931. Lamennais, who had decided in favor of the separation of Church and state, read it, erroneously, as being a criticism of the Concordat's system. But, on the contrary, this historic treatise on the relationship of Church and state fully recognized the merits of the Concordat (1801-1802), which made the Church a protectorate, dependent on the state.

Having finished this treatise, Dom Guéranger, with Lamennais's encouragement, returned to the work that had preoccupied him since his seminary days: a book on the decadence, and restoration, of ecclesiastical studies in France. But, once again, another interest intervened, and the study lay dormant; only vestiges of it can be found in several articles published in 1832 in the *Tribune Catholique* under the title, *On theology.*

For some time, in fact, a new subject had come to absorb Dom Guéranger. Newly enriched by his training as a writer, he was being led, all unconsciously, to realize the purpose of his service to the Church. He was being called to give back to France one of the great traditional institutions of the Church, surpassing all scholarship in magnitude and service.

"In the course of the spring of 1831," recounts Dom Guéranger, "the newspapers inserted in their want ads the sale of the Priory of Solesmes, which they listed as an abbey. The news left a deep impression on me. This landmark, so beloved of my childhood, vulnerable, perhaps, to some strange turn of events. . . . "

The priory was purchased in 1791 by Henry Lenoir de Chantelou. In 1812, M. de Chantelou went all the way to the Emperor Napoleon to ensure that the statues in the church, coveted by the prefect of la Sarthe for the cathedral, would remain at Solesmes. Soon thereafter, in 1825, the priory passed into the hands of three rich property owners in the region. They tried, vainly, to make it profitable in a variety of ways— as a minor seminary, glassworks, warehouse for slate from Angers, and so on. The monastery was even in danger of falling into the hands of "the black gang," men who didn't hesitate to turn the most cherished landmarks into profit-earning quarries of stone.

On learning of the sale, Dom Guéranger hurried to inform Abbé Gerbert, a disciple of Lamennais. But Lamennais had concerns of his own and was not interested in the priory.

"As the announcement about Solesmes continued to appear in the newspapers," Dom Guéranger explains, "I couldn't tear my mind away from the thought of that house being saved and utilized. All of a sudden, near the month of June, the idea came to me that if I could gather several young priests, we could reestablish there the Order of Saint Benedict, with the divine office and studies. My duties to the bishop and my stay in Paris had suspended the aspirations I had had in the seminary. They suddenly sprang to life again, and have never since left me."

The suddenness of this inspiration cannot be overemphasized. Dom Guéranger had naturally wished more than once to see the Benedictine life in France restored, but he had never imagined that he would be the instrument. Now, through a fortuitous event, he was filled with resolution, one that human motivation alone could hardly explain.

More remarkable still, the idea of a foundation came at a time when he was immersed in the study of Tradition. This circumstance was to mark his monastic work profoundly, for Solesmes was to be a promoter of the authentic spirit of tradition in the Church.

At first glance, the project seemed utopian. Like the other religious orders, the Benedictines in France had no legal rights, no freedom, no citizenship. As noted, the Revolution had made religious life illegal; the "commitments" involved in such a life were regarded as being "contrary to the natural rights of man," as it was officially put.

Napoleon, in his day, had also turned against the monks, whom he considered "useless," a religious aberration unheard of in apostolic times and therefore presumably unnecessary. His official support of Catholicism was cynical and arbitrary. His second Organic Article of 1802 suppressed all ecclesiastical establishments other than cathedral chapters and seminaries. Portalis, minister of Worship in the Empire, put an end to all discussion with one sentence: "The century of monastic institutions is passed." These words, unfortunately, reflected opinion in general; the term "monk" had come to evoke obscurantism, a denial of progress. Only a few cultivated spirits still looked for the resurrection of the learned Benedictine monks of Saint Maur—the great scholars in traditional Church history, who had left many works unfinished.

As it happened, under the aegis of royal authority, a faint hope for the Church had appeared during the Restoration. But by reclaiming the protection of the civil power, the Church would abjure her rights and the dignity of the great religious orders. Despite these drawbacks, the Benedictines chose this course in 1816. At that time, Dom de Verneuil, last prior of Saint Denis, was able to reunite several former Maurists at Senlis, where they took up their regular religious exercises and teaching activities. But at his death and due to the secular behavior the monks had adopted during their twenty-five years of exclaustration, the attempt to bring the traditional monastic life back to France floundered.

From that experience, it seemed that, to be reborn in France, Benedictine life had to wait for a new generation, free in spirit from the *Ancien Régime* and consequently more apt to pick up the thinking of Saint Benedict and adapt it to new times.

The year 1831, however, was hardly a favorable time for this renewal. Nor was the strongly Catholic region of western France, astir with legitimist (royalist) agitation, the best area to attempt the revival of an institution still associated with the

French monarchy. The events at the Trappist monastery of Melleray, in the diocese of Nantes, were still fresh: in the beginning of October, some monks had been dispersed, and the abbot, Dom Antoine de Beauregard, thrown in prison. The policies of the Regime of July 1830 held little hope for religion in the country.

Apart from the political situation, personal considerations weighed upon Dom Guéranger, but they did not deter him either. Thirty years later, he would recall this time quite simply: "My youth, the complete lack of temporal resources, and the limited reliability of those with whom I hoped to associate—none of these things stopped me. I wouldn't have dreamed of it; I felt myself being pushed to proceed. I prayed with my whole heart for the help of God; but it never occurred to me to ask his will concerning the projected work."

What gave him such great assurance? "The need of the Church seemed to me so urgent, the ideas about true Christianity so falsified and so compromised in the lay and ecclesiastical world, that I felt nothing but an urgency to found some kind of center wherein to recollect and revive pure traditions."

Although the program was obviously vast and imprecise, his reference to the Church does not imply a preoccupation with arcane matters or nostalgia for the past, but rather concern for the Church of his time. He was convinced that the role of the monastic orders was indispensable to the Church.

III

THE BEGINNINGS OF SOLESMES

DURING THE TWO YEARS THAT PRECEDED the renewal of Benedictine life at Solesmes in 1833, Abbé Guéranger marshalled all his energies toward his goal, but without anxiety or feverish activity.

One month after deciding on the project, he was able to return to his beloved priory. At the invitation of the Cosnard family (one of whose daughters, Euphrasie, had chosen him as her spiritual director in Le Mans) he arrived in Sablé in July of 1831. There he met an assistant pastor, Abbé Auguste Fonteinne, a year older than himself. He took him, along with his hosts, to visit the endangered priory, but without disclosing his plans for the place.

That walk was fraught with emotion. The world of those statues, so expressive, was filled with the ambiance of peace that every visitor feels on entering the old silent church on a summer's day. The scene at Marmoutiers was repeated, but this time the *Rorate* was sung by the two priests. There were more visits during the following days, but still the young priest kept his secret. Before leaving, however, he inquired discretely about the possibilities of a religious community there.

Abbé Guéranger did not inform his friends of his plans until November, on his return from a retreat at la Trappe de Port-du-Salut near Laval. Surveying the facade of the priory house, he confided to Abbé Fonteinne his wish to found "a house of prayer and study" there. Fonteinne's response was unexpected and encouraging: he wanted to help. While short on learning, he could bring his heart and his two strong arms to the enterprise. As for the Cosnard family, their generosity was moving.

Heartened by these responses, Abbé Guéranger left immediately for Paris to consult with the team at *L'Avenir*, above all with its chief, whose word would be decisive. Lamennais received him on November 13 at eight o'clock in the evening. After hearing him out, he declared: "Nothing could be more in harmony with the needs of the Church. Nothing could more aptly regenerate the ecclesiastical sciences in a solid and lasting manner."

But Lamennais, founder of a Congrégation de Saint Pierre, objected to the large role that communal singing of the Divine Office would play in a life dedicated to study. P. Guéranger tried to explain: the emphasis on the choir was precisely what had made him choose the Benedictine Order. Lamennais persisted: "How could you make this form of life attractive in a century of action such as ours?" Because, Guéranger said, "we wish above all to live the life of the Church, without bowing to the tastes and habits of our contemporaries." Lamennais embraced him.

"The matter of legitimacy being thus forever settled," P. Guéranger wrote to Abbé Fonteinne on the day following this historic meeting, "the only remaining question is application;

that is to say, to find the means to realize a project that the greatest man of the century believes is important."

Most important, he had to submit the project to the bishop of Le Mans. "Mgr. Carron," wrote Dom Guéranger, "relished what I said about the need to regenerate the study of Catholic traditions and to employ the help of a congregation to that end; he applauded the idea of reviving the Order of Saint Benedict, with its respected and scholarly memories, its large and proper rules that can bend to the needs of the times. He seemed undeterred both by the circumstances of the moment and the material difficulties."

But the bishop—knowing that P. Guéranger was held in the diocese to be "the dance master of Lamennaisianism," and that Solesmes would be suspected of being a second La Chênaie (the mansion of the de Lamennais family)—decided to wait for the verdict from Rome that was being sought by the "pilgrims" of *L'Avenir*: Lamennais, Montalembert, and Lacordaire. Abbé Guéranger hoped, naively perhaps, to obtain from the Holy See an official letter of encouragement, which would put an end to Monseigneur Carron's hesitation. He went so far as to give Montalembert (January 1832) a letter to deliver to Gregory XVI. But the moment was poorly chosen. As Montalembert explained to his friend, Rome was dealing with governments as timidly as ever.

Undeterred, P. Guéranger continued his work on a study on faith, which he envisioned as a prelude to a vast "work of theological renovation designed to repair the state of ecclesiastical teachings." Despite the depressing uncertainties, he never wavered, as his letters to Euphrasie Cosnard show: "I am beginning to believe that it is truly God who has inspired me with certain ideas, and, that being the case, that we shall overcome difficulties (if any arise) by storm. . . . But it is prayer above all that we need. Pray then; get others to pray;

let us pray, and with a right, pure, and sincere intention, with a spirit of self-denial and sacrifice, searching for nothing but the kingdom of God, secure in the knowledge that all the rest will follow. . . .

"Let us not forget, if we do succeed, if our plans—much greater than our reach—indeed come true, we must always say from the bottom of our hearts that we have been, and are, and always will be, useless servants. Finally, in the midst of the impulsive enthusiasm that besets us before such great and beautiful things, and whether we succeed or not, let us not forget that it is all the same in the eyes of God. Mankind's drunken nature judges his work by success. God, better at appreciation than man, examines the intention and looks for nothing but that; the intention comes from us and from his grace; the success comes only from him."

Thirty years later, Dom Guéranger recalled these thoughts: "My prayer was humble, and I am able to say that appearances, in any sense whatsoever, counted for nothing with me." Burying himself in a small country priory, the former Parisian, who might well have enjoyed a promising career in the capital, turned his back on honors.

On August 15, 1832, the encyclical *Mirari vos* condemned the liberalism of the Lamennaisian school. On September 20, Abbé Guéranger sent his bishop a letter showing his complete compliance with the Church's dictum. He then congratulated Lamennais, in his eyes a true champion of the rights of the Holy See, on his presumed submission. But instead, on November 30, he received a harsh response, and was thus constrained to cut off his relationship with Lamennais. He never, however, indulged in recriminations, in contrast to some disciples of La Chênaie.

Meanwhile, the acquisition of the priory of Solesmes had become urgent; tired of waiting for a buyer, the owners had begun to demolish it. To halt the vandalism, P. Guéranger hurried to rent it. He submitted the names of several priests who promised their cooperation to Monseigneur Carron and received his assent to the project. Concurrently, the monastery of the Visitation of Le Mans was asked to begin a novena of prayer on December 7 for its success.

"In the first days of this novena," recounts Dom Guéranger, "I was praying in the chapel of the Visitation. I was called interiorly to consecrate the work of reestablishing the Benedictines in France to the Sacred Heart of Jesus, to which I had consecrated myself in the chapel of this same monastery on Maundy Thursday in 1823. I vowed to ask the bishop to allow me to have in Solesmes a benediction of the Blessed Sacrament in honor of the Sacred Heart on the first Friday of each month once we were established, and to erect an altar to the Sacred Heart in the church of our monastery, if three years after our installation we could continue the work."

Before the end of the novena, on December 14, the lease was signed at Sablé. Dom Guéranger never forgot his ride from Le Mans to Sablé on a decrepit horse over snow-covered roads. He recalled the exclamation of a woman who saw him cross the village of Saint-George: "Oh! *Monsieur le Curé*, how poorly mounted you are for a priest! What a lumbering beast you have between your knees!" But laughter aside, the passages in the Gospel about the man who wished to build a tower, and the requirement of poverty for the true disciple, came to him in a strange way during the trip. Already poor, what more must he give, he thought anxiously. "What happened afterwards," he would say at the end of his life, "taught me what further privations God would exact of me in return for the honor he was doing me in my work." Several days later, Bishop Carron approved the little Regulation prepared by Abbé Guéranger for the

"Regular Association Established in the Diocese of Le Mans under the Protection and Good Wishes of Monseigneur the Bishop"—the official jawbreaking title of the first community of Solesmes. It could not be called Benedictine as yet, for it had neither been affiliated with an existing monastery nor had it received the investiture of the Holy See. It nevertheless strove to live in every way according to the Rule of Saint Benedict.

Instead of attempting to observe every strict detail of the Rule, Abbé Guéranger decided to incorporate its essential lines and to borrow from the practice of the former Saint-Maur congregation. He attenuated the thousand-year-old observance on two points only—abstinence of meat and rising during the night—quite well aware of the responsibility he was assuming. The Trappist abbot of the Melleray, Dom Antoine de Beauregard, regretted the mitigation, but acknowledged its inevitability. But Dom Lecomte, a former Maurist retired in Nantes, was more positive: he felt the program was wise, which comforted the future prior.

Having acquired the priory and received the blessing of the bishop, P. Guéranger devoted the remaining six months before the official installation to material preparations.

Rarely has something been taken over so unostentatiously. The evening before, January 2, 1833, Abbé Guéranger quipped to his companion, the abbé Fonteinne, "Let's go ask for hospitality from the *choubiaux*" (the cabbage-patchers, the old gardener and his wife, guardians of the priory). "Tomorrow, we'll wake up in our own house." Fonteinne, who had decided to join the restored Order despite the distress of his parishioners at the nearby village of Asnières, loaded his baggage onto a cart drawn by a horse lent them by the marquise de Juigné. The cart contained several utensils and two coarse mattresses, one for an old pallet in the grand parlor of the monastery for use by the future abbot, the other for the cellarer in the petit parlor.

Once settled, the abbé Fonteinne busied himself with repairs, building fences, recruiting local handiwork, and procuring a few beasts, while Abbé Guéranger took the pilgrim's staff. His long letters, punctuated by moments of incredible verve, give a picturesque account of his outings. These included Laval; Nantes, where the marquis de Régnon put him in touch with Lamennaisians who were devoted to the project; and Melleray, where Dom de Beauregard promised him the help of two of his religious and gave him the advice of long experience. But insofar as fund-raising was concerned, the result of these trips was pitiful.

On March 21, in the parish church of Solesmes, Abbé Guéranger sang the Mass of Saint Benedict for the first time; his companion acted as cantor before an old Roman Gradual in-folio. The entire congregation consisted of two elderly women and an unexpected guest, Edmond de Cazalès, who had come to prepare an article on the sculptures of the priory of Solesmes for the *Revue Européenne*. Abbé Guéranger helped him—and the study ended up by giving an account of the work of the new Benedictines.

The principal service rendered by Edmond de Cazalès, however, was his mention of Madame Swetchine, the only person in Paris, he said, who might possibly be interested in the restoration. Armed with a letter of recommendation, Abbé Guéranger left for the capital, where he stayed for three months.

From her very first interview with the little priest from Le Mans, Madame Swetchine, the famous Russian convert, understood the importance of the work of Solesmes. A spiritual friendship immediately sprang up between these two— an older woman, whose keen sense of the greatness of God allowed her to grasp the importance of monastic life, and a much younger future Benedictine, whose openness, zeal, and learning ignited her devotion.

In her salon on the rue Saint-Dominique, Madame Swetchine received many of the Catholic elite; she related to many young men, such as Montalembert and Lacordaire, as a mother. But it was from the young prior of Solesmes that she sought counsel, and to him that she submitted her spiritual writings—a somewhat paradoxical situation, which she enjoyed.

Over and above the moral support of such a personality, Dom Guéranger gained strength from her humble and persevering dedication, without which he could never have interested the salons of Parisian society in "The Work of Saint Benedict," a charity that would sustain the Benedictines through annual subscriptions of five francs.

While in Paris, Abbé Guéranger also went to visit Abbé Desgenettes, who invited him to preach in the famous sanctuary of Notre-Dame-des-Victoires where Desgenettes had been pastor. And he again saw his old friend, the printer Bailly de Surcy, the "father of young people," who was the prime mover in founding the Conférences de Saint-Vincent de Paul; he, in turn, was enthusiastic about an enormous printing project that would be taken up at Solesmes. "Father" Bailly also took on the mission of recruiting monastic vocations.

Abbé Guéranger continued his begging. On one occasion, he personally thanked Chateaubriand for his December 1832 letter—later famous—in which the needy writer promised a donation of 40 francs. (Had Victor Hugo, the poet, been home, would he too have contributed?) In contrast, a former Maurist, Dom Groult, whom Dom Verneuil had named trustee of quite a large sum earmarked for a monastic restoration, would not donate any of it to Solesmes on the grounds that it was not oriented to teaching. "But when God pushes, nothing stands in the way," was the response of Dom Guéranger to this, and all disappointing news.

But the good that proceeded from the 2,500 francs he garnered with such tremendous effort was as nothing compared to what came from the acquaintances he made or renewed in Paris and at the Grand Collège de Juilly. Many priests, such as Abbés Gerbet and de Salinis, were also deeply taken with "Roman" ideas, and later they went on to the episcopacy.

Whatever the difficulties, the abbé's confidence was never shaken. He went to the Sisters of Saint Thomas de Villeneuve to pray to the black Virgin who had come from Saint-Etienne-des-Grés and had delivered St. Francis de Sales from the temptation of despair; from that moment on, Dom Guéranger never again felt the least anxiety.

(Unfortunately, Abbé Fonteinne had found no such serenity. During the three months Guéranger spent in Paris, he carried on his own practical fight alone on the banks of la Sarthe, caring for fifteen animals and driving himself crazy with thoughts about the impending inaugural date.)

In drafting a prospectus to announce the renewal of Benedictine life at Solesmes on July 11, 1833, Abbé Guéranger took into account the mentality and prejudices of his time. He recalled the good things attained by the monks of the past through manual labor, studies, and an apostolate that built up Europe in the Middle Ages. Given the short time since the Revolution, it was impossible to do more than throw out platitudes.

(An amusing sidelight: the publication of the letter of Chateaubriand in which he was identified as an "honorary Benedictine" gave rise to rumors that the elderly man was going to retire to Solesmes.)

The ceremony of July 11, on the feast of the Translation of

Saint Benedict, commemorating the removal of the saint's relics from Monte Cassino to France, marked the return of the monks to their home after forty-three years of exile. At the singing of the psalm *In convertendo* (Psalm 126, When the Lord turned again)—the psalm of the exiles' return—a group of thirty priests accompanied the first eight "monks" from the parish church to the priory. The Mass was sung *"au Romain"* (in the Roman style) and an old confessor of the faith from revolutionary years, Canon Ménochet, who represented the bishop, celebrated the resurrection of a venerable Catholic institution. During the course of the ensuing meal, the *Life of Saint Benedict* by St. Gregory the Great was read.

"Starting from vespers on this great day, the Divine Office has never been interrupted in our church," Dom Guéranger later wrote. (The various expulsions of the monks did not occur until the end of the century.) The day before, benediction of the first bell had taken place, and the bell was placed on top of the roof of the priory. Following this ceremony, Abbé Guéranger was elected prior by his companions, the abbés Fonteinne, Daubree, Jouanne, and Leboucher. With them were the four lay brothers who had also joined. Of this first community, only the prior and the cellarer would persevere in the monastic vocation.

The new Benedictines had to wait three years before adopting the habit. They wore the cassock and, to accustom the population to the reappearance of the monastic cowl, they went out wrapped in a great cape with a pointed hood. Finally, on August 14, 1836, for first Vespers of the Assumption, they came down into choir with the tunic and leather belt. Dom Guéranger took the scapular and the cowl from the altar, donned them, and gave the habit to his companions.

The news provoked an influx of the curious for Sundays

to come. In their joy, the monks showed themselves proudly: Dom Fonteinne began going to market in his cowl, according to the old monastic custom; not to be outdone, Dom Gourbeillon, on his way to Précigné, mounted the monastery's donkey whose rump disappeared under the billowing folds of his habit.

The daily life of the first years, in buildings out of which chunks had disappeared, was filled with work, although the needs of the monks were fewer than today. Still, the paucity of monks necessitated a doubling up of duties. Their humble means, the rural way of life, and a bit of fancy, all contributed to confer an ambiance on the Solesmes of this era that had its charms, as well as its inconveniences.

In the course of the first weeks following the installation, Dom Guéranger wrote enthusiastically to his friends: the old church resonated anew with the chanting of the psalms; the monks, with but one heart and one soul, showed not the slightest fatigue (he himself was amazed at his own stamina); he no longer had time to study, but, no matter, the entire community would take on the task.

Still, Dom de Beauregard, the abbot of Melleray, was far from optimistic. His response was gloomy: "All establishments have their honeymoon, their initial fervor." He went on to describe the somber future of a monastery. With no traditions, directed by a prior with no experience, it would inevitably run into insurmountable difficulties as the various temperaments went to work on diverse interpretation of the Rule. "You will find yourself obliged," he continued, "to deal this poor Rule so many chisel blows, that I don't know if Saint Benedict would be able to recognize it." It was his way of criticizing the softening of the observance which Dom Guéranger had deemed indispensable.

The misgivings of Dom Antoine in respect of governing

the new monastery soon proved justified. A humiliating revolt against the prior—fomented by several callous youths—jolted the monastery in the spring of 1836. It could have been the death of Solesmes—the second attempt (Senlis had closed down twenty years earlier) to revive the Benedictine Order in France. During Dom Guéranger's absence, the prior was "deposed" by his community—no more than ten at the time. Monseigneur Bouvier, who came to put things back in order, had the best explanation for the incredible incident: "My poor Father, with what brains are you surrounded!"

Dignified and gracious, Dom Guéranger kept his sufferings to himself, hoping to forget the gross ingratitude of his fellow monks; but he underwent moral solitude for years.

Even before the installation of 1833, various people had wondered, somewhat reproachfully, why Dom Guéranger did not back himself up with several former Benedictines. He had, actually, a small dossier of letters from thirteen veteran Benedictines in eleven different dioceses written between 1833 and 1838. Nine had belonged to the Congregation de Saint-Maur, two to Cluny, and two more to Saint-Vanne.

All spoke of their joy and sent their best wishes for the success of the little monastery. Eight of them, wishing to die in a house of the order, asked for information about entering and the observance, and wondered if they were the only ones to take this step. But behind their requests lay a hidden and understandable unease: the youngest were septuagenarians. At Solesmes, the oldest was less than thirty-five years old.

One veteran Benedictine, Dom Chabbert, canon of Tours, after taking stock of his infirmities, told Dom Guéranger sensibly, "I think that the small number of religious who, professed from different congregations, compose the

Benedictine Order in France, will be absolutely useless for the same reasons that I advance."

To renew is not to break with the past. Convinced of this, Dom Guéranger was filled with admiration for the reform of Saint-Maur and the fruits it bore. His doubts centered on its centralized organization, as well as its doctrinal deviations, which had tarnished the reputation of its last members in the eighteenth century. Although in restoring Benedictine life he surrounded himself exclusively with men of his own generation, he did borrow lavishly from Saint-Maur in elaborating the Constitutions of Solesmes.

As a sign of this spiritual filiation, Solesmes accepted from a benefactress a pastel portrait of Dom Ambroise Chevreaux, the last superior general, killed in the Carmelite massacre of 1792, a seal of the Congrégation de Saint-Maur, and a large antiphonale of Saint-Germain-des-Prés.

When Dom Guéranger restored Solesmes, he did so quietly. The press nevertheless covered the events of July 11, 1833, in a series of articles that evoked diverse reactions.

The publications devoted to Lamennais, as well as French and Belgian Catholic journals, rejoiced at the news. In other reactions, L'Ami de la Religion smelled a subversive group of Lamennaisians at Solesmes. La Gazette de France and the Journal des Débats were respectful, Le Figaro made fun of it, Le Constitutionnel denounced it as a "sacerdotal invasion," Le Courrier Français found that "it was falling backwards quite a way to return to Saint Benedict," and L'Europe Littéraire regretted that, for lack of anything better to do, the modern spirit had to accept such antique institutions.

To the official and scientific world, more interested in intensive studies than monastic prayer, the Benedictines of Solesmes looked like new Maurists. The concept of the "learned Benedictine," of the monastery as the "refuge of science and virtue," won for the priory the goodwill, or at least the neutrality, of groups that usually had little interest in Church doings. At the French Institute, as at other learned centers, no one hesitated to seek help from Dom Guéranger and his erudite colleagues who helped him in his research.

This slightly precocious reputation traveled all the way to M. Guizot, then minister of Public Instruction. In early 1836, he entrusted some work to the monks at Solesmes, whom he considered the rightful heirs of Dom Mabillon and Dom Montfauco; it was the completion of *Gallia Christiana*, a history by provinces of the dioceses and monasteries of France, undertaken by the religious of the Saint-Maur congregation.

Montalembert, who saw this as "the opportunity for Solesmes to find a place, governmentally, politically, scientifically," in France, pressed Dom Guéranger to accept. After some hesitation, the prior did so and drafted a memo on the work. It was, of course, beyond the strength of one man, but the annual stipend of 4,000 francs would be enormously helpful.

Two years later, "M. Guéranger, director of the House of Studies of Solesmes"—the government addressed the monks by this social circumlocution—learned that the new minister, M. de Salvandy, ill-informed about the exigencies of the work in question, had decided to cut off funds.

In le Maine, the old adage would be repeatedly proved true: a prophet is without honor in his own country. Aside from a few friends, the work of Solesmes encountered nothing but indifference, or hostility, because of the reputation of Lamennais. "We are a new Port-Royal," Dom Guéranger wrote Madame Swetchine (August 9, 1833). "The word is out: crush Solesmes. And then the Comité Royaliste de Paris, which denounces us in the provinces as a dangerous obstacle to a legitimate restoration, and then, and then. . . [But] God is

with us, that much is certain. Here we are, some truly inof-
fensive men, quite silent on our rock cliff; in the one month
since we have been established, we have had time to do
nothing but our Offices; meanwhile, in the plain below, we are
parodied; we are exaggerated; we are represented as hostile
and menacing."

Even more mortifying was the ignorance of their neighbors, exemplified by the remark, "What a shame this beautiful
house isn't lived in!" This convinced the monks of how easy it
was to remain hidden. Madame Swetchine wrote along these
same lines to Dom Guéranger in 1838: "Solesmes will live a
long time in the shadow of the affection of a few, and in the
indifference of nearly all."

An outpouring of correspondence stands witness to this
affection. It sprang mostly from those who eagerly sought
signs of a Catholic renewal. During this time, the friendship
between Dom Guéranger and Charles-René de Montalembert
deepened, a friendship of two brothers-in-arms, filled with
the same passion for the freedom of the Church and unity
with Rome. They were both intelligent and enthusiastic; and,
beyond this, the prior had a feeling of spiritual fatherhood
toward his friend, a caring for his soul. The young peer of
France, for his part, was filled with the impetuosity and
romance of chivalry, an innate taste for greatness and beauty,
and an understanding of the monastic life that Dom
Guéranger deeply loved.

During Montalembert's stay at the priory in autumn of
1835, he prepared his biography of Saint Elizabeth, was
baptized on the evening of October 31, and generally participated in the Office in the monks' stalls. There were also the
long conversations with the erudite prior—and his own playfulness; one day he took two little kittens into the refectory in
the pockets of his frockcoat and had them make the sign of the

cross. All these youthful doings wove links of brotherhood between the two men.

Without the intervention of such friends, Solesmes would quite simply have died of starvation. The list was long: from the marquis de Dreux-Brézé, who offered the first 500 francs, to Montalembert, who gave part of his modest fortune to the monastery, to the women of Sablé—"our good women," Dom Guéranger used to say—who could be seen on the road to the priory hefting heavy baskets in their arms. And this took courage in an era when monks were considered useless oddballs. But these women, some of whom had hidden "truant" priests during the revolutionary years, understood that the spirit of God was at work in this little corner of Sabolian earth.

IV

CONFIRMATION

AWARE THAT HUMILITY WAS INTEGRAL TO HIS WORK, Dom Guéranger tried to avert any talk of himself. He was reluctant at first to ask Rome for official approbation of the restoration of Solesmes, as his Parisian friends, principally Mme Swetchine, were pressing him to do. "You have to be a baby before you can be an adult," he would say, referring to the infancy of his monastery, "and, besides, not all children grow up." It seemed better to wait and present the Holy See with a work of some proven stability. But despite his demurrals, an initial step was undertaken in 1835. And it failed.

The following year, on July 11, 1836, the members of the community at Solesmes took their vows for five years instead of annually. The little rule of 1833 was also rewritten and incorporated into the constitution.

Vocations were still not too numerous, but they appeared to be firmer than the initial ones; the government, moreover, seemed to be looking benevolently on Solesmes. As a consequence, Montalembert, in Rome where he had gone after his marriage, contacted Dom Guéranger. Was it not time, he asked, to assure the monastery more security by leaping over the threshold into adulthood—to try once again in Rome?

Montalembert himself helped prepare the way for his friend by enlisting a number of notables in the cause. Dom Guéranger asked him to prepare Rome on one particular point—his appearance: despite his youthful looks, he was, he insisted, almost thirty-three years old.

Finally, on February 12, 1837, Dom Guéranger left Solesmes, accompanied by Father Charles Brandès, a convert from Lutheranism and friend of Montalembert. The trip took on the aura of a pilgrimage: a stop-over in Le Mans at the Church of Saint-Benoît; another at Notre-Dame-des-Victoires in Paris. After a stay in the capital, they left for Marseille, visiting Auxerre, Fourvière, and Notre-Dame-de-la-Garde on the way. At Marseille, the travelers embarked for Genoa and Livorno, where Dom Guéranger, with whom sea travel did not agree, proceeded by land to Rome. When he reached Florence, he was disappointed to discover that he had missed Montalambert by a matter of hours.

On Holy Saturday, March 25, at 5:00 in the morning, Dom Guéranger arrived in the Eternal City. He went straight to St. Peter's and laid the dossier put together for the Vatican's approval, as well as the key to the monastery, on the steps of the Confession (the burial site of the apostle in the basilica below the main altar). His prayer took on an extraordinary intensity: he felt he was at the center of the Christian world, at the core of the Church's unity. "Dom Guéranger's soul," remarks Dom Delatte, "was able to savor the taste of triumph that the faithful feel when in Rome at St. Peter's."

So as not to anticipate Rome, the prior wore the dress of a secular priest rather than his Benedictine habit. He made many pilgrimages to the sanctuaries of Rome, of course, but his main tasks were to call on numerous prelates and to correct the text of the constitution.

In short order, Dom Guéranger won over the redoubtable Cardinal Sala, prefect of the Congregation of Bishops and Religious, who was known to be averse to the proliferation of new congregations in France. At the same time, he had to resist the inducements of the abbot of Saint Paul Outside the Walls, Dom Bini, who hoped to turn Solesmes into a renovating branch of the Benedictine Congregation of Monte Cassino. Dom Guéranger, however, held fast to his freedom: "We will do nothing without our monastic independence. . ." His reaction was open and friendly; it simply expressed his resolution, no matter the hurdles, to return to the original spirit of St. Benedict.

The cause of Solesmes found its warmest partisans among members of the Society of Jesus. Two names stand out: Father John Philip Roothan, the Father General whose cause for beatification would be introduced in the twentieth century, and Father Rozaven, consultant for the Congregation of Bishops and Religious. The latter had turned down the first request for approval of Solesmes in 1835 because of the monastery's Lamennaisian reputation. But this time around, Don Guéranger succeeded, though not without difficulty, in reassuring him and other opponents that Solesmes was neither Lamennasian, nor Gallican, nor yet Jansenist. His work on the *Origines de l'eglise romaine,* supposedly put together by the community of Solesmes which he had carried hot off the press, served as a certificate of orthodoxy.

On April 11, the prior of Solesmes was finally received by the Pope. In the course of the audience, Gregory XVI let it be understood that he would not allow the title of Congregation de Saint-Maur to be taken up again. It was, of course, the very title Dom Guéranger wanted to adopt, precisely to show that he only sought to restore an institution already approved by the Church. Although the prior believed that the Maurinis' true history was poorly understood in Italy—they had undoubtedly left an impression of doctrinal deviations—Dom Guéranger bowed before the will of the Pope. He therefore proposed the title Congrégation de Solesmes, but Rome preferred Congrégation de France.

This may have been the result of an uneasiness in the Holy See, which was very careful to maintain good relationships with world governments, about the position of Solesmes vis-à-vis the French government. Advised of these fears by Montalembert, the Marquis de Latour-Maubourg, ambassador of France, undertook to alleviate them.

One of Dom Guéranger's major concerns was to do away with the alterations in the familial order that had taken place in Benedictine monasteries during the course of the centuries. The spiritual fatherhood of the abbot had in particular suffered from being modeled after those of centralized congregations. In the process, abbatial perpetuity had given way to a system of triennial change, which had become so common that a number of high personages in the Roman court believed that Saint Benedict himself had instituted it.

As a result, it took true courage for Father Rozaven to affirm, in his report in favor of Solesmes, that the perpetuity of abbots was one of the essential elements of the Benedictine Rule. In another section he gave the reasons why it was necessary to raise a house as young as Solesmes to the status of an abbey.

To prevent his cause from bogging down, Dom Guéranger arranged for it to be submitted to a cardinal's commission of seven members, each one of whom he had to visit and cultivate. As the day of decision approached, the prior wrote to his monks to redouble their fervor in prayer.

On the evening of July 9, while he was on his knees before the Madonna of the Via delle Botteghe Oscure—a miraculous Madonna who cried tears in 1796 during the occupation of Rome by the French troops of the Directoire, and whose feast was on that day—he heard the carriages of the cardinals passing on their way to the Quirinal to pronounce on Solesmes. Later, he returned to Saint Callixtus, a house belonging to the Benedictines of St. Paul, where he had taken lodging.

Before midnight, someone came with the news: all his requests had been granted. The constitutions had been approved; the Benedictine Congregation of France was recognized as the spiritual inheritor of the ancient Congrégations de Cluny, de Saint-Vanne, and de Saint-Maur; and the priory of Solesmes was raised to the status of an abbey, with Dom Guéranger its abbot—a benefice he had not asked for. But the perpetuity of his abbatiate would not become effective until after three triennial scrutinies, and he would be the only abbot of his congregation to enjoy this right.

To this day, Solesmes faithfully memorializes July 9 by celebrating the Virgin under the title *Mater Providentiæ*; it also, of course, celebrates July 14, 1837, the day of the official birth of the congregation, the day it received its Apostolic confirmation.

Dom Guéranger obtained the approbation remarkably fast. This could have been because he proposed merely to restore the eldest and most venerable of the religious orders in a land where it had once flourished, and, once restored, simply to follow the Rule of Saint Benedict. Still, the official nod given to the resurrection of the Benedictines in France was surprising, given the scruples the Holy See had about promoting an institution that had no legal status in the eyes of the government of Louis-Philippe.

Lacordaire, Dom Guéranger's companion in Rome, wrote to Mme Swetchine: "M. Guéranger is perpetual abbot of Solesmes, having ring, miter, and crozier, and head of the Congregation of Benedictines of France, affiliated to Monte Cassino. This is a marvelous event, one that must lead us increasingly to love the Roman Church, so divinely clever at discerning her true sons." Dom Guéranger, for his part, was profoundly moved: Through the words of the successor of Peter, the Church had pronounced on his work; Solesmes had received the mission to lead and propagate monastic life in France according to Saint Benedict; Solesmes was recognized as beneficial to the Church; Solesmes would therefore survive all difficulties, present and future.

From now on, it behooved the new abbot to enter fully into the family of Saint Benedict. At the conclusion of a ten-day retreat, on July 26, the feast of Saint Ann, Dom Guéranger read his Charter of Profession before the altar of the sacristy in the basilica of Saint Paul Outside the Walls. The basilica itself had been inaccessible since the fire of 1823. The French colony of Rome was present, and Lacordaire's joy was complete. The abbot of the monastery, Dom Bini, who juridically received the vows, spoke of Ezechiel's vision of the dried-up bones recalled to life: "*Ossa arida, audite verbum Domini* (Dry bones, hear the word of the Lord)." The newly professed abbot later said, with a grin, that he had never really felt dried up.

Following the ceremony, nothing seemed more fitting than that he immerse himself in the atmosphere of the places once frequented by Saint Benedict. Monte Cassino was too far, but Subiaco was the site par excellence of monastic youth. Dom Guéranger left Rome on July 27.

The impressions he received in the savage valley of the Anio, and, above all, at Sacro Speco, where he passed a part of the night in prayer, were profound. On the thirtieth, during his first pontifical Mass, he received the profession of Father Charles Brandès and took for the theme of his allocution a verse from the Book of Tobit: "*Filii sanctorum summus* (We are the sons of saints)." He emphasized the continuity of the work of God throughout the ages. Above all, his words expressed his joy and humble hope: Solesmes was founded on the rock that carried the Church—on Christ, on Saint Peter, and finally on Saint Benedict. "This new congregation," he said once again, "cannot have any life other than that of the Church."

Dom Guéranger planned to return to France via Rome. But a cholera epidemic broke out and closed the borders. He also had to wait for a recalcitrant copyist to finish the Brief, *Innumeras inter*, in which the text of the constitutions appeared. During his wait, he had a farewell audience with Gregory XVI (August 12), and finally, on September 1, the Brief was signed.

But by this time, weakened by the Roman summer and months of exhausting work, Dom Guéranger's strength failed; he, in turn, was struck by cholera and owed his cure to the ministrations of his friends, most notably Lacordaire. The sickness was quickly under control, but not without leaving its marks: all his life, he was subject to frequent attacks of fever, at times triggered by a simple ray of sunshine.

During this time, the monastery was in the throes of formidable material difficulties, exacerbated by the prolonged absence of the prior, which disturbed the creditors. Dom Guéranger tried to solve the problems, but the distance—it took a month for word to pass back and forth—made it difficult. Yet he retained his good humor and encouraging tone: surely the tribulations were a sign of God's blessing. What, after all, was there to fear, once the Church had pronounced on the subject? "Though it were necessary for me to die and be buried here," wrote Dom Guéranger, sensing his illness in advance, "the work of God would nevertheless continue on its course, because the oracle of the Apostolic See does not speak in vain, but very much through the prompting of the Holy Spirit, and sooner or later his words must be fulfilled."

Finally, on September 25, six months after his arrival, he left Rome, accompanied by Lacordaire. It took fifteen days for them to get to Milan, after which they crossed Switzerland and called on Montalembert, who was living in Villersexel in the Franche-Comté. But despite the happy reunion, the new abbot's thoughts were focused on his abbey. When he arrived in Paris, he placed his Roman correspondence in the hands of Count Molé, minister of Foreign Affairs, and refused to ask for an audience with the king, since doing so might have been interpreted as seeking the approval of the civil power.

Dom Guéranger's return to Solesmes, on the eve of All Saints Day 1837, had a profound effect on those first monks; they were aware that a new era had dawned. Over and beyond the joy of seeing the abbot again, they took great pride and hope from the thought of their future role in the Church, and many of them began to keep a chronicle of life in the monastery.

The monks had been discussing how to solemnize the arrival of their abbot but, in the end, it took place quite humbly. Coming by way of Notre-Dame-du-Chêne, Dom Guéranger got out of the carriage at the entrance to the village, donned his pontifical insignia, and entered his abbey to the sound of bells, while his monks accompanied him singing the psalm *In convertendo* (Psalm 126, When the Lord turned again). In the choir, one of them read the Brief, and the first Vespers of the feast were celebrated without a backward glance.

The news soon spread throughout the region. At first, people came out of curiosity: a Benedictine abbot seemed such a strange sort of person. But, little by little, the nave of the abbey church emptied, visitors became rare. Leon Landeau, the young owner of the marble factory of Solesmes, was often the only attendee at the Offices, along with a blind man. This latter prompted a remark from the neighbors: "They have such beautiful ceremonies at the monastery, but there is only a blind man to see them."

On November 21, 1837, Dom Guéranger received the four first professions, those of Fathers Fonteinne, Ségretain, Gourbeillon, and Osouf. In exchange, each of them received a medal given by Gregory XVI, as well as a copy of the Rule. These vows, ending the novitiate, were solemn.

The first few months of Dom Guéranger's abbatiate at Solesmes had barely ended when a great discord arose between him and Bishop Bouvier. What has been called the "quarrel of the pontificalia"—the dispute concerning the insignia of a bishop and monastic privileges—is one of those affairs that at first glance seems to be the fault of both parties. But further examination draws a different picture.

It would be tedious to go into detail, but the central facts are these. On November 27, 1837, Dom Guéranger, with what he believed was Monsignor Bouvier's assent, presided at the clothing of a novice at the Carmel in Le Mans, only to discover later that the bishop had taken umbrage, not having given his explicit permission. In asking Dom Guéranger to officiate without it, the prioress had acted imprudently.

In the way of background, Monsignor Bouvier had always encouraged and even protected the Benedictine monastery. He had denied that it had any leanings toward the doctrine of Lamennais, lent it money, officiated in an ordination in 1834, and so on. But his somewhat authoritarian temperament and his administrative mentality made discussion difficult, especially when he believed his rights were in question. Whether or not he was Gallican (the term is filled with ambiguity), it remains that he did not grasp the significance of religious exemption.

Dom Guéranger, on the other hand, understood it well; it was, he knew, essential to the existence of a religious order. And as he himself was intransigent in matters of principle, it would have been impossible for him, however politely, not to have firmly resisted the bishop's contention.

An exemption of this sort partially removes an individual or a community from local episcopal authority and places him or it directly under control of the Holy See. It thereby manifests the right of the Pope directly to exercise his jurisdiction over all the faithful and underlines his universal and sovereign power over Catholics; in consequence, it becomes a sign of the unity of the Church. But the bishops of France had become unaccustomed to this privilege, so incompatible with the "maxims" of the Gallican Church, and now Dom Guéranger was determined to reclaim it.

It is also possible that Dom Guéranger's youth—he was just thirty-two—had aroused some jealousy among the entourage of the bishop of Le Mans, engendering such questions as, are there now going to be two bishops in the diocese? The conflict at first extended only to the insignia (the pectoral cross, crozier, and miter) as well as to the number of pontifical services in the liturgical year (only a few feastdays). Monsignor Bouvier, for his part, insisted on regulating their use inside the monastery and forbidding them outside it. Dom Guéranger, with arguments based on law and history, tried tactfully to enlighten him. A rash of letters flew between Solesmes and Le Mans, but it was a lost cause: each side repeated the same arguments over and over again. Finally, in September 1838, Dom Guéranger yielded to the extent of submitting the affair to Rome.

During the disagreement, the abbot met with incomprehension, even disapproval, from certain of his friends, who feared that the strife would attract the government's attention and thereby endanger the existence of the monastery itself. They tended to consider the pontificalia as no more than symbols of dignity, which monastic humility should in any case be willing to sacrifice. These people were unaware that during the first years of his abbatiate, Dom Guéranger, far from playing the prince, waited on his monks at table on the very days that he celebrated pontifically. He therefore explained to them the profound and imperative reason for his stand on the importance of signs: at stake was the legitimate independence of religious orders and, through it, Roman authority, which Gallicanism was striving to limit.

Did the religious orders have the right of citizenship in the Church of France? Or, as Monsignor Bouvier seemed to think, were they no more than institutions analogous to diocesan congregations? The bishop, using the nonrecognition of solemn vows by civil legislation as a pretext, refused to acknowledge them—that is, to accept them as inviolable commitments to a religious family exempt from his jurisdiction.

At the height of the conflict, Lacordaire came to Solesmes for a rest (June 20-July 12, 1838). The preceding year in Rome, Dom Guéranger had vigorously encouraged him to restore the Order of Saint Dominic in France. Lacordaire had been moved, but before reaching a final decision, he wanted to make a long retreat near his Benedictine friend. Lacordaire's correspondence seems to establish that the advice given him then by Dom Guéranger was the deciding factor.

Although very different in temperament, the two men thought highly of each other. Primarily, they agreed about the role of religious orders in the Church and in society; both wished to enhance the freedom of the Church in France and saw in the religious habit a sign of that independence. Unfortunately, the excellent relationship between two of the principal artisans of the Christian renewal of the nineteenth century suffered from the liberalism and political positions which Father Lacordaire espoused in the late 1860s.

Having finished his retreat on the banks of La Sarthe, Lacordaire, the future Dominican, decided to do something about the reputation of the abbot, which was suffering from his contretemps with the bishop. Traveling to Rome, he explained to the Roman congregations what was really going on in Solesmes and Le Mans. "Nothing is harder for a Catholic heart," Guéranger wrote, "than ecclesiastical persecution."

Rome was lavish with its counsels of peace. But since the difficulties arose every year at ordination time, Dom Guéranger was forced to return to Rome himself during the summer of 1843 and obtain a document upholding the rights of religious superiors. In the end, he procured a Brief that conferred upon him the privileges belonging to the abbots of Monte Cassino, reputedly blessed by the Pope, with the right to confer minor orders.

At this point, Monsignor Bouvier got in touch secretly with the government, which at the time was extremely displeased with certain religious congregations for circumventing episcopal jurisdiction by dealing directly with Rome in defiance of the Organic Articles. The French Chamber of Deputies had been ringing with the diatribes of Messers. Dupin and Isambert against the Dominicans, the Jesuits, and the Benedictines—specifically, the Benedictines of Solesmes—who, they claimed, were sowing division among the clergy by agitating the liturgical question, instead of making themselves useful to society like the Trappists, the Chartreux, or some other congregation that indulged in commercial activities. The political atmosphere was equally troubled by the controversy over the freedom to teach.

Given the turmoil, and the Holy See's quiescent attitude, the minister of Worship (Ministre des Cultes), M. Barthe, proposed that Monsignor Bouvier dissolve the community of Solesmes. But the bishop protested that he didn't think such an extreme measure necessary, that it would suffice if the French ambassador to Rome showed some firmness.

Although the Holy See refused to reveal the Brief *Inumeras inter* to Paris, since the French Council of State might have declared it contrary to French institutions, it withdrew from Dom Guéranger the rights conferred on him in 1843. Solesmes, once again, became subject to diocesan jurisdiction. The news reached the abbot at the beginning of 1845—total defeat after seven years of battle.

For Dom Guéranger, this blow was an opportunity to attain true greatness. Far from rebelling, or even from submitting publicly and indulging privately in recriminations, he wrote his monks from Paris, and, while making no attempt to hide his pain, explained this new event, which seemed to augur a diminution of the Church's freedom.

"Our congregation," he said, "suffers persecution, and the most cruel kind of all; for the authority of the Apostolic See is at the moment being exercised against her [Solesmes]." And he explained how Rome was forced to cede because of French threats made against the religious orders. This defeat notwithstanding, he remained faithful to Rome.

"We have confidence," he concluded, "that such trials will not diminish in the least the attachment you all profess for the rights of the Apostolic See. You love Rome because of St. Peter and St. Peter because of Christ: nothing, therefore, is changed. Our common father believes it is necessary, for the sake of peace, to throw us into the sea. Jonah did not perish in this test: on the third day he saw the light again. Let us have confidence and cry out to God: the day of Resurrection will come."

The response of the monks at Solesmes matched their abbot's. The entire community was strengthened by the trial, and Dom Guéranger rejoiced: "I was greatly consoled by your persevering love for the Holy See. It is the sign and vital principle of the Congregation. This spirit could not in reality exist in us without trial."

Compared to the blow the Jesuits received in 1773, he remarked, Solesmes' travails were trivial. Its activities had barely been constrained. "Let us therefore be sons of obedience, always faithful, more than ever: there, I repeat, is the glorious mark of true Regulars."

Such fidelity could not help but make a profound mark on the future of this religious family. A great hurdle had just been taken: put to the test, the structure, founded on the rock, had proved unshakable. The temptation to revolt or to despair was routed. When other tempests came—and Solesmes would be hit by more than one—the memory of Dom Guéranger's courage and fidelity in 1845 saw them through.

Throughout, a great friendship had helped the abbot of Solesmes to bear the weight of the battle: that of Mgr. Nicole Fornari, nuncio to Paris since 1843 whom he had met in Rome in 1837. This prelate had immediately perceived the role the "Regulars" would play—to gather a clergy still impregnated with Gallican traditions and return them to the unity and universality of the Church. Such perspicacity, said Dom Guéranger, was not very common in Italy, where the problems of the French were not always understood. It was in part thanks to Monsignor Fornari that the measures of 1845, suspending the legitimate rights of the abbot, were retracted in 1852, only seven years later.

The year 1845, however, did not end without Dom

Guéranger undergoing a yet more humiliating trial, one that broke him physically, but one from which he learned. In 1841, he had decided to found a house in Paris. Monsignor Affre, the new archbishop, seemed receptive to the idea, an attitude that lasted not much more than a year. Dom Guéranger wanted to spread the Congrégation de France, which could thus, little by little, escape the tutelage of Monsignor Bouvier. Solesmes could count upon solid friends in the capital, and, besides, the studies of the monks called for increasingly frequent trips to the great libraries.

"We will have more and more tasks that necessitate a stay in Paris," wrote Dom Guéranger to Montalembert. "Now, it seems clear to me that monks would run great risks there if the house they lived in, even temporarily, were not a monastery where they could immerse themselves in obedience and the practice of divine service and monastic exercises. I speak to you according to my conscience as abbot." In January 1842, Dom Guéranger leased a building on some land on rue Monsieur that had long ago belonged to the abbey of Saint-Germain-des-Prés, and it was outfitted, after a fashion, as a monastery.

But he made the mistake of confiding the management of the house to a young priest, Father Etienne Goussard, who had money in the Americas and was inclined to think of himself as a business tycoon. His fantastic projects captured the imagination of two successive superiors of the little priory of Saint-Germain, Dom Paul Piolin and Dom Jean-Baptiste Pitra, although they were not totally blind to the rather unmonastic behavior of their energetic cellarer. As for Dom Guéranger, he naively thought it sufficed to protect Solesmes by not using his own signature to business transactions, but simply giving his permission to his subordinates to proceed as they saw fit.

In one month, Père Goussard acquired the Hôtel de Montmorency-Laval in Paris and an immense property at Bièvres, in the diocese of Versailles, the whole for the sum of 750,000 francs. Partial resales, all were told, would guarantee a profit. Dom Pitra assured Dom Guéranger that his Parisian friends were delighted that he was finally free of financial worries. In the meantime, loans were made and huge construction projects began. Before long, the cellarer was deeply in debt, at the mercy of unscrupulous bankers.

Meanwhile, believing that his foundation was in good hands, Dom Guéranger asked Rome to recognize it as early as 1843. Happily, the Holy See refused. Soon thereafter, in September 1845, the abbot of Solesmes, despite his efforts, saw the collapse of the house, which brought on an onslaught of creditors, the discovery of Père Goussard's corrupt administration, and the withdrawal of the monks from Paris and Bièvres.

Aware of his imprudence, Dom Guéranger strove to minimize the wrongdoings of his religious and take the blame upon himself. Many of his friends, even some of his monks, who had warned him of the danger, pointedly reminded him of this. His letters to Montalembert showed the depth of his suffering and humiliation. He would have gladly sacrificed his life to undo the damage. "God never has need of a man, and when one man is lost, it is not a great loss. The misfortune in all this, the unique misfortune, is to see a whole religious order compromised and, by extension, all the others."

During this dark hour, Solesmes was saved by a group of devoted friends, headed by Monsignor Fornari: he vouched, in person, for the honesty of the abbot of Solesmes, and under his aegis the Avouerie was founded, a rescue committee to sustain the Benedictines of France. The principal members were the Count de Montalembert, and Messrs. Baudon,

Thayer, and de Kergorlay, the latter two lending huge sums. A young lawyer, M. Lesobre, took the business in hand and was able to limit the damage.

This sad experience caused Dom Guéranger to reflect. He did not give up his plans for the great monastic studies, but he felt he should first form his monks more profoundly, to prepare in this way for the future foundations of Solesmes.

One of the unforeseen consequences of the setback in Paris was to make Solesmes more widely known, both in France and abroad. As a result, the rescue committee pled with Dom Guéranger to send several of his monks to collect funds throughout the provinces.

Dom Eugène Gardereau headed for Brittany, which he plodded over for months on end, pulling his horse "Smiley" through muddy roads, knocking at rectory doors, yet somehow finding the time to participate in a polemic with the *Annales de philosophie chrétienne*. His success as a mendicant often depended on the attitude of the clergy toward the Roman liturgy: the name Dom Guéranger immediately brought to mind the *Institutions liturgiques* that had recently created such a stir. Before long, Dom Gardereau acquired a reputation as a preacher of retreats and of the Stations of the Cross during Advent and Lent; by the end of his life, all of the dioceses of France knew him.

Dom Pitra prospected in the east, with far less financial success, but, as will be seen later, with singular success in uncovering manuscripts, which led him to places outside of France. Other monks covered the central and southeastern parts of the country. As one result, Père Camille Leduc, future founder of the Servants of the Poor, after manifesting his talents as an administrator, was sent to take care temporarily of the community of Andancette.

Andancette. The name must have stirred sad memories

for Dom Guéranger, for it was tied to the affair of the Saint-Germain priory. Around 1843, after much hesitation, the abbot of Solesmes had consented to assist spiritually a small convent of ten "religious" near Valence. He visited the house twice and left a monk, Father Nicolas-Brémon, there as chaplain. These efforts, however, were resisted by the superior, an intransigent and tyrannical woman with a volatile temperament. By 1847, the matter had so escalated that the bishop of Valence closed the convent. Unfortunately, Père Goussard had borrowed quite large sums from the superior, who proceeded to proclaim far and loud that the poor sisters had been gulled by the Benedictines. She had, in fact, run into debt herself. Despite his liberal reimbursements, she brought Dom Guéranger to court, and, against all expectations, won her case in 1853. Once more, the benefit committee saved Solesmes.

At this time, the abbey was just barely beginning to recover from the financial collapse of 1845, which had been exacerbated by the economic crisis of 1848. All in all, Dom Guéranger had lived through some painful times. Despite his confidence in God, despite his natural serenity and optimism—the sort that allowed him in the midst of his troubles to edit such works as L'Année liturgique—he felt frustrated. He confided only to a number of his intimate friends, but the monks noticed that within several months his hair grew white.

Among the many turning points in Dom Guéranger's thirty-eight-year abbatiate one surely came in the mid-1850s—a time that brought a sense of improvement, a sort of stabilization. Solesmes and its abbot seemed to have moved to an era of greater peace after a relatively agitated period.

But the change should not be exaggerated. Previously, neither the quarrel of the pontificalia, nor the difficulties of the

Parisian foundation, nor certain local malicious charges prevented the monastery from proceeding with its peaceful life. And poverty always prevailed; it would stalk the abbot of Solesmes until his death. (Other, more painful trials, to do with his foundations and with some of his religious, were still in the future.)

But from the vivid documents of the abbey during this time—the second half of the nineteenth century—a feeling of consolidation emerges, of a better established rhythm and regularity. There are many reasons for the increased stability. First, Dom Guéranger's abbatial authority had become more properly recognized both inside and outside the monastery. For the new generation of monks, he was a prominent man; and he himself showed more circumspection in admitting postulants. Moreover, after his return from Rome in 1852 as perpetual abbot, his governance, no longer submitted to triennial scrutiny, took on an air of stability.

In addition, the difficulties with Monsignor Bouvier began to dissipate, particularly after December 1851, when Dom Guéranger was named a consultant to two Roman congregations. With age, the bishop became a little more conciliatory. At his death in Rome in late 1854, the position of Solesmes in le Maine changed: Mgr Jean-Jacques Nanquette, the new bishop of Le Mans, publicly expressed his esteem for the monastery and its abbot.

Many factors converged to benefit the monastery—the regard in which Dom Guéranger had come to be held in France because of his works and his perseverance in the face of adversity, the Brief obtained by Monsignor Gousset, archbishop of Rheims, from Pius IX in 1851 recommending the work of Solesmes to clergy and faithful, and the return of the country to political stability and economic prosperity in the Second Empire.

But it is impossible to evaluate other influences, which only Dom Guéranger, by virtue of his position as founder, could reveal. He was too sensitive to the expression of God's will in these events, not to understand that the trials of the past years were meant to purify, enlighten, and confirm both himself and his whole community. His goal did not waver, but he understood that he must bide his time humbly before seeing it realized.

* * *

To continue Dom Guéranger's life in a purely chronological manner would diminish it and even risk giving a false picture of his personality and life; to depict a monk in his monastery allows for more latitude. The best method, then, is to begin by looking at what constituted the center of Dom Guéranger's life—what gave it unity—and then to see how his diverse activities, his relationships with the other monks and his friends, his personal labors, and so on, revolved around this center.

At this point it would be fruitful to stop for a moment and consider Dom Guéranger as a person—to destroy old legends and discover new realities. The black bindings of *L'Année liturgique* that used to stand in a line on the shelves of family libraries gave a very uninteresting picture of their author. Certainly this was the impression received by Monsignor Fayet, bishop of Orleans. After a lesson in liturgy, the bishop confided to a Jesuit priest, a friend of Dom Guéranger, who afterwards repeated it to him, "I imagine the abbot of Solesmes as tall and thin."

"Pardon, Monseigneur, he's actually rather short, and more stout than thin."

"But at least he must be dark, with very black hair, a

severe sort of air, stiff."

"I'm sorry to say, bishop, that Dom Guéranger is very blond, with blue eyes and a constant smile, and that he's very happy and loveable."

Dom Guéranger was five-feet, five-inches tall. After having retained his youthful looks for years, he began in his fifties to put on some weight, as seen in the portrait painted by J.-E. Lafon in 1865, which shows his two small, plump hands. He had a fairly powerful and bony head—his "square head," as he would jokingly say—the front high and large, crossed by heavy oblique wrinkles descending towards the left; his eyes, which were intensely blue, and his clear and lively gaze tended to surprise people.

Happiness was one of his most striking characteristics. It came through, not as joviality, but as a sort of playfulness, full of humor and an infectious warmth; his quick wit and laughter were pervasive.

Simplicity and greatness were also noticeable—traits he considered the special marks of St. Benedict's work. Perhaps the former quality was most striking in his person, whereas the second generally characterized his writings. He had a horror of posturing, of looking for an effect. His love of self-effacement did not, however, spring from timidity, which never bothered him. Rather, he had the calm assurance of strength, of those who never care about their popularity because they are firmly anchored in the truth.

Dom Guéranger undoubtedly had a fiery temperament, but he gave the impression of poise, of a solid equilibrium. "He did not like," said Monsignor Charles Freppel, "the violent and redoubtable states of soul, where one exaggeration calls to another. Neither brusqueness nor harshness could emanate from such a gentle and firm spirit." If his letters are energetic and sometimes pressing, they carry no sense of feverishness, anxiety, or nervousness. Even their penmanship is revealing. In sum, he was vivacious without being short or distracting; he knew how to take his time—"ever busy, never in a hurry," as Louis Veuillot put it.

Dom Guéranger's artistic sensibilities seem to have been sparked principally by what we call today the plastic arts; his travel notes swell and take on life whenever he describes a church or museum. Architecture—such as the English cathedrals and St. Cecilia in Albi—above all evoked his enthusiasm. But in respect of painting and sculpture, his interest lay principally in their expression of religious ideas, in the artists' message, rather than in their technical qualities. His reflections on *The Assumption of the Virgin* by Murillo, which he considered the best of all masterworks, are revealing in this regard.

He had more difficulty with music. Though he played no musical instrument, he could appreciate the performance of a pianist or an organist who happened to pass through the monastery. A later chapter will deal with his stunning aesthetic sense concerning Gregorian chant. And as for poetry, Dom Guéranger had been attracted to it from his youth and his vision of the world would always be colored by it.

Yet another abiding trait of Dom Guéranger was his love of variety, his horror of monotony, of any military-like uniformity. This trait is tied to another—his attachment to freedom, to independence. This is not to imply that he was a nonconformist; it is to say that he disliked the blind submission to current fashion that transformed human beings into sheep, senselessly repeating conventional formulas. Whenever truth was in doubt, Dom Guéranger "did not fear," said Monsignor Freppel, "to swim against the current of opinion rather than let himself be swept away by it."

In 1875, Charles Louvet left to Solesmes the several letters he had kept from his old childhood friend. To them, he added some pungent notes that perfectly illustrate this portrait sketch of Dom Guéranger: "These letters, filled as they were with his rich and vigorous nature, were recognizably his even without his signature. In them you will see with what ardor and perseverance Guéranger pursued his friendships. His heart was on a par with his spirit; and spirit and heart were joined to a very strong character. God evidently created him to organize and to command. But he also gave him a very vivid imagination, which, while adding great charm to his letters and his conversation, made him somewhat ill-suited to long and continuous work. He only liked to work at his own pace, and the thing he detested most, apart from sin, was a task imposed on him that had to be completed within a fixed time.

"He had true independence of character, that is to say, the kind that bows respectfully before great authority and bends with difficulty before lesser powers. Several months before his death, he spoke to me, still with juvenile indignation, about the miseries that the study masters put him through at the Collège Royal in Angers, and for which he never forgave them. Monk and abbot of a monastery, he bore the Rule of the house cheerfully because it came from God; but had it come from another, he wouldn't have stood it for twenty-four hours. He made an excellent Benedictine; he would have been a terrible soldier.

"But what above all distinguished him was the sureness and depth of his faith. There is where the unity and the glory of his life are found. Never could any man say more than he: my soul is built upon the Lord."

V

THE ROMAN CHURCH

As January 30, 1875, dawned, the thought that prevailed among Dom Guéranger's friends was that they had lost "a great servant of the Church, an indefatigable champion of the rights of the Holy See." This feeling stemmed primarily from his writings, notably the *Monarchie pontificale*, which crowned his body of work.

But, in truth, Dom Guéranger's entire life—all of his activities—was praiseworthy. Since space disallows an in-depth study here, we can only take a cursory look at some of the writings that epitomize his thoughts and works.

From the very first, Dom Guéranger was drawn to the Church and all that touched the Church. His family background, shaped by the grave events that affected French Catholics during the Revolution and the Empire, his youthful reading, and the Lamennaisian movement that perturbed the clergy, all without doubt moved him. But over and beyond these influences, the young priest reached his own synthesis, his own discovery; and this suffused his entire work.

A passage from his autobiography speaks of his discovery—the superiority of the Roman liturgy over the Gallican version which had been composed in France in the eighteenth century. It came at a time when he was close to immersing himself in dry erudition. But, now, this newly found treasure—the Roman liturgy—made him "go more and more deeply into the inmost consciousness of the Church." His ensuing research of "general ideas" opened the door to a contemplative view of the Christian mysteries; the Incarnation appeared to him as a sun, in whose rays the whole mystery of the Church burst into light.

Dom Guéranger's fundamental intuition concerning the Roman liturgy, which he gained as early as age twenty-five, developed on two levels: theologically and apologetically. The first predominates in *l'Année liturgique*. In it, the Church is presented as the bride of Christ, after the great Biblical image found in the writings of the Fathers. For Dom Guéranger, the Church is, above all, a living person indissolubly linked to the Son of God in his role as intercessor. And so, in his writings, he speaks movingly about her, or to her, in the prayers he formulated for each of the saints' feasts.

He finds joy in living the entire liturgical seasons praying the prayer of the Church; he exults in her holiness, which shines in her glorified sons; he brings to light her universality, her unity—she is the perennial Spouse "ever young and without wrinkle" and, finally, he marvels at her freedom, for she draws her being and her rights from none but God alone.

Dom Guéranger would have loved to do nothing but go deeper and deeper into this theology, like a contemplative. But circumstances soon threw him into apologetics; and as war makes more noise than peace—and controversy is inherent in apologetics—he gained an unwanted reputation as a polemicist. It was impossible for him, complete monk that he was, to see the image of the Church being distorted without intervening, without using to their fullest, the gifts God had given him on the Church's behalf.

But in order to take up for the Church, he had to come down to earth and face his adversaries. These, the Gallicans, had narrowed the concept of the Catholic Church to nothing more than a human society that must respect the "rights" of the Gallican Church. In defining the juridical relationship between the Gallican and the Roman churches, they had succeeded in cutting off their ecclesiology from its life-giving sources.

Gallicanism (and Jansenism) in France, like Febronianism and Josephism abroad, led to disaffection with the papacy: it was no longer seen as anything but a power that must be limited; its vital role in the Church was lost from sight.

Aware of these evils, the abbé Guéranger at first countered them solely intellectually: "I saw only one thing," he stated, "that the very structure of the Church had to be saved from the aberrations to which Gallican teaching had subjected it." Thanks to his deepening theological thought, to his continual study of the Fathers, and, above all, to the daily practice of the liturgy, he succeeded in his scholarly dispute; that is, he established the supernatural reality of the mystery of the Church of Christ.

A good example is his *Monarchie Pontificale*. This book is a compilation of unfinished essays, the first of which, drafted in 1853, has a significant title: "Roman Thought on the Hierarchy and its Relationship with the Purity of the Faith." Dom Guéranger believed that faith was totally important. Gallicanism seemed dangerous to him precisely because, in diminishing the unity of the Church, it endangered faith and therefore the work of Christ.

A second essay, written a little later, is entitled: "Formation of the Church by Jesus Christ, and the Essential

Characteristics with Which He Imbues It." In it, Dom Guéranger continues to propound his main line of thought on the unity of the Church, a unity for which he never stopped fighting.

The Word, he maintained, became Incarnate to gather the human race back to God, uniting believers into one unique and universal family: the Church. The Church, for its part, has no greater task than to keep faith alive in the hearts of its members. Dom Guéranger contends that there can be no unity of faith without unity of the Church. And the unity of the Church, modeled on Trinitarian unity, cannot exist without a unifying principle: Christ, who is cornerstone, doctor, and universal pastor. As the Church is a visible society, so its principle of unity must equally be visible.

Now, as we know, ever since the Ascension, Christ has been invisible. But, in conformity with the economy of the Incarnation, he wanted to keep himself visibly present, and this he did in the person of Peter, and has done thereafter in the successors of Peter to the See of Rome. What Christ would do invisibly for the Church, the Pope does visibly.

The bishops, by virtue of their "episcopal" character—Dom Guéranger was already using the term—are "cooperators of the Pope in service to the unity of the Church." If the Pope reserves certain rights to himself, it is for the good of this unity.

Dom Guéranger never confused unity and uniformity. The Church, he held, was a most diversified organic body, but one in which the members did not live except by being joined in the principle of unity.

Having come out of the disruptive eighteenth century, Dom Guéranger felt it was imperative for Catholics to recall the essential unity of the Church. In a vital reaction to schismatic elements, which he shared with his entire generation, Dom Guéranger saw that such hard times required an awareness of this fundamental feature of the Church. "The Church," he wrote, "as she advances across the centuries and moves further away from the days when the uncreated Word resounded through the earth, has an increasing need to feel in herself the vigor of the principle that keeps her and makes her live."

Just as pontifical sovereignty serves the unity of the Church—the Church being herself at the service of the faith of her members—so pontifical infallibility is tied to the infallibility of the Church. The abbot of Solesmes defended this infallibility in powerful words—not, unfortunately, well enough known. He showed that the Church was infallible in her teaching and in her practice, notably in the liturgical expression of her faith. Against false conceptions of tradition or "progress" held by this or that segment within the Church, he strongly illuminated the truth and demonstrated its permanence, from the very origins of Christianity through its every development. This fundamental thought can be found in most of the abbot's works, a thought that, coincidentally, Newman was illustrating at the same time.

One page from the *Memoir on the Immaculate Conception* demonstrates Dom Guéranger's firmness and clarity: "If one could assign a period, however short it might be, during which the Church might cease to be under the influence of her divine author, during which she would be deprived of the guidance of the divine Spirit which he poured down upon her, it would mean the failure of the promises of Jesus Christ; the whole edifice of Christian faith would collapse from the base.

"It can easily be seen that one of the faithful, whose personal existence does not even stretch over an entire century, need not search through all the ages that have preceded him to know what the Church teaches. The Church of his time responds to him according to the doctrine of past centuries and the doctrine of centuries to come. Otherwise, how could he, alone, possibly have a sufficient appreciation of her teaching, across so many generations? He believes the Church (*credo Ecclesiam*), and with this faith, he is in intimate communion with the Divine Word and with the Holy Spirit, who did not abandon this Church for even one day which They have deigned to establish as their necessary instrument for the salvation of the human race.

"It is therefore dangerous to divide the life of the Church into periods, when it comes to her teachings. The Church is always the same, in whatever period one considers her.

"What Tradition is, is the Church herself believing and professing such-and-such a doctrine; and the witnesses of that doctrine, the monuments of her length of days, of her existence in time, are valuable only in that they represent the thinking and the teaching of the belief of that changeless society. If in one century the symbols seem more developed than in some other, that only means that the Church, by the movement of the Holy Spirit, who directs her, has judged it fitting to make more explicit, for the benefit of her children, that which was in her from the beginning; and we know that she is divinely assisted in the work of this development.

"What difference does it make if, in the wake of the destruction of milestones from ancient centuries, we cannot always trace the precise step of some particular dogma through the ages? Our zeal to collect the witnesses of the Fathers must not slacken because of it; but should we happen to lack these witnesses of the past, is mother Church not there to supply us with her firm and dazzling light of which the Fathers are but a few scattered rays, whose value is only in their reflection of her, their center? The Church, always divinely assisted, always vigilant, always pure, always 'without spot or wrinkle,' believes today what she believed yesterday, what she will believe tomorrow, but she perceives it and teaches it with an ever-greater clarity and precision."

Dom Guéranger discerns an extension of the Church's charity, along with her dogmatic development:

"It took many generations for the treasures of light, deposited by Christ inside the innermost memory of his Bride, to see the dawn of day, just as the treasures of charity which he entrusted to her needed centuries to pour out over the world, in proportion as new necessities called for new helps and new resources that the preceding age had not even suspected. God alone knows the measure of doctrinal development and charity he has prepared for his Church, for he alone holds the secret of the duration of the world, which he created for her alone."

The constancy of the Church as an institution also draws Dom Guéranger's attention. The continual development and renewal of the Church do not, of course, affect her fundamental structure. Her constitution, because she was given it by God alone, can never be compared with this or that worldly constitution, as some attempt to do. To wish, for example, to bring the parliamentary system into the life of the Church is to misjudge the very character of her being, her hierarchy.

As a man of the "century of revolutions," Dom Guéranger was eager to demonstrate the contrast between the permanence of the Church and the vicissitudes of nations and states. He had known numerous people of the *Ancien Régime* who regarded the revolutionary period as the end of the world. He himself lived under six different political systems and saw France shaken three times by revolution. Without dwelling on the reason for this instability—the abandonment of Christian law—he jumped at the opportunity to introduce his readers to the one indestructible city. He marveled at the steady succession of popes over the past eighteen centuries. Surely, this was reason for hope. As early as 1831, he cried, "The Church alone remains standing, while thrones totter!"

To Montalembert, frightened by the troubles of 1848, he sent these lines: "The old society has no more place in history. We march toward unknown regions. But in this breakdown, it is comforting to think that the Church remains; she grows greater from all that falls around her."

When French troops abandoned the papal states and many feared for the future of the Church and her leader, Dom Guéranger reassured his friends; in simple, short phrases he summed up his faith—"God watches over his Church, I fear nothing for her"—and recalled the "promises" made to Peter. This one word summed up the reasons for his confidence.

The freedom of the Church was perhaps the cause that first fired the enthusiasm of Prosper Guéranger, faithful reader of the *Mémorial Catholique,* a Catholic review edited by M. Gerbet (later a cardinal) and the organ of the school of Lamennais. Undoubtedly, his own independent spirit made him react sharply to any limitation of the Church's rights—an affront, as he saw it, to the Church's dignity. Once again, he discovered in theology the basis for this freedom: sovereignty. That is, because the Church draws her being from no one but God, the Church is independent of all temporal authority.

L'Année liturgique, consecrated to the heroes of ecclesiastical freedom—Hilary, Gregory VII, Anselm, Thomas of Canterbury—is firm in tone and content. The author details the areas where sacred freedom must be exercised in complete disregard of all secular power: teaching, the administration of the sacraments, the evangelical counsels, relations among the hierarchy, the development of institutions, the administration of temporal goods. In all these areas, and many others, the Church in France was being shackled.

Was Dom Guéranger, then, opposed to the Concordat and

a partisan of the Separation? To believe that would be to misconstrue his thinking, for he clearly distinguished between the spiritual and the temporal; he taught that the Church and the state, each sovereign in its own order, must buttress one another. In the historic reality of nineteenth-century France, he maintained, these principles were imperfectly respected. But if the Church is limited by restrictions, this does not nullify "the true principles"—her freedom in her own sphere as ordained by God himself.

In regards to civil power, the abbot of Solesmes was loyal: But "for him," D. Delatte wrote, "only one political program existed: the interests of the Church. His heart went out immediately to any regime that understood that, in the words of St. Anselm, nothing was dearer to God than the freedom of his Church." Even when the state brushed aside the rights of the Church, as it did after 1858, Dom Guéranger remained loyal to it, "supporting the power as the power," although he continued to deplore its abuses.

As a rule, he refused to become mixed up in political discussions; he saved his strength for other matters. "All my life," he wrote in 1869, "I have lived outside political parties; I have never served any cause other than the Church." He asked his sons to do the same.

All this having been said, he had a weakness for the Bonapartes and argued amicably with his friend, the bishop of Poitiers, over the legitimist tendencies of the prelate. But Napoleon III's sudden change after Plombières' interview with Cavour about the future of Italy in 1858 tempered his enthusiasm, and the Bonapartes in 1870 left him unmoved. Many in the community at Solesmes wanted him to embrace the cause of the comte de Chambord, which he at first resisted; when he finally did give in, it was more out of kindness than conviction.

The abbé Guéranger felt he could well spend his entire life defending the rights of the Church through his writings, although he tended to wear himself out when he felt the truth was in danger. "Polemics rob me of the little strength left to me," he wrote during the controversies on papal infallibility, "but the cause of the holy Church needs to be upheld." He chose that fight even over the one to save his house, his monastery, whose very existence was threatened at the time he warred against Gallicanism. As for the calumnies leveled against him personally, he never bothered to contest them.

Serving the Church in this way was an honor, a grace, that evinced generosity, purity of heart, and union with Christ. In a letter he wrote, "Love for the Sovereign Pontiff is a mark of God's blessing, just as a coldness in this area shows that faith is languishing." In this same spirit, he paid homage to the Pope in all of his works.

Had he remained a secular priest, with more free time, Dom Guéranger would undoubtedly have developed his themes more completely. But God asked him to serve the Church in a more fruitful way than writing on subjects of evanescing interest. Dom Guéranger, in the end, fashioned a more lasting book; he engraved his thinking in the hearts of his monks; he transmitted to Solesmes his zeal for the Church; he made his sons and their successors witnesses to those aspects of the Church which he wished to impress on his contemporaries.

Divine praise—the supreme function of the Church—was practiced at Solesmes before it ever appeared in *The Liturgical Year*. Moreover, in adopting the Roman liturgy from the very first, in 1833, the new Benedictines demonstrated their dedication to Catholic prayer and their respect for apostolic authority.

The unity of the Church thus found a defender in the

monastery. As shown in a prior chapter, in respect to monastic exemption from diocesan government, the religious, by their mere presence, witnessed in favor of Rome's supremacy over Gallican pretensions. "Each day," wrote Abbé Guéranger to Montalembert in 1832, "when we preach the doctrines of the Holy See, we hear that we have no mission to do so…. It is high time for the creation of a holy and canonic opposition, which Rome has laid down among the privileges of Regulars [religious exempted from episcopal jurisdiction and under papal control]. The Regulars, disseminated throughout the Church, are the protectors of the Holy See, the disinterested and alert sentinels, always ready to raise their voices to uphold the rights of the common Father, without curtailing in any way those of the episcopate."

After the revolutionary epoch came to its inevitable close, the continuity of the Church and her dedication to holiness became apparent with the reestablishment of Benedictine monasticism—the ideal evangelical life, ancient as the Church herself. Archbishop Gerbet of Rheims emphasized this point in his 1851 mandate supporting Solesmes: "By its mere presence, the Benedictine order attests to the strength and fecundity of the Church's institutions; it is a witness to its perpetuity, and to its prescription."

Finally, even under the rule of a Concordat, which set itself up as sole judge of the usefulness of religious orders, the Benedictines of Solesmes were a visible affirmation of the freedom of the Church. They refused to ask for governmental sanction or to reclaim their legal existence—and they wore the habit openly, even in the streets of Paris.

As for monastic activities, the intellectual work of the monks was at the disposal of the Church: her needs determined the direction of individual or conventual efforts.

Solesmes was, as Dom Guéranger put it, "a school

devoted to the Holy See," not as a supplementary vocation, but as the monastic vocation itself. This conception was so new to his contemporaries that in 1838 Dom Guéranger described his monastery as "the only French house whose very goals and fundamental laws of establishment are exclusively Roman." In its Constitutions of 1837, he made this explicit.

Inasmuch as the Church's good demanded unity, it was in being "Roman" that Solesmes showed itself "faithful to the Church." Dom Guéranger himself always maintained this ideal: "Today," he wrote in 1859, "whether one says Rome or one says the Church, everyone understands it to be the same thing, because everyone knows that Rome cannot be on one side and the Church on the other."

But to remain content with nice-sounding declarations was not the abbot's style. Nothing was more important to him than to infuse in his sons the same force that animated him: an unshakable faith in the Church, an ardent and intelligent love for her, and a constant interest in her undertakings. "Monastic life," he said, "without love of the Church, without submission to the Church, is a horrible temptation to pride." On one occasion, referring to certain Maurist Gallicans, he said, "They took great pride in their observance, were quite attached to their exercises, and very pious in their manner; but more secularity surrounded them than in a good old, slightly relaxed abbey where the Church is really loved."

The joys and sufferings of the Church were echoed at Solesmes; the abbot would comment on them in his lectures or prescribe a conventual prayer for them—as, for example, exalting the freedom of the Church when in 1837, the archbishops of Cologne and Posen were arrested for resisting the Prussian bureaucracy.

As for submission, we know his own example of it in 1845.

In fact, as far back as 1833, he had spoken clearly on this point in a letter addressed to *L'Ami de la religion,* which had accused Solesmes of still being a bastion for the condemned ideas of Lamennais: "We require of all our brothers a total submission to all the decisions and all the teachings of the Apostolic See." This was inscribed in the Constitutions of 1837.

The best guarantee for the monastery's survival, he believed, was its dedication to the Church. "Solesmes will not be lost," the abbot said one day to Madame Swetchine, "so long as Rome declares it useful to the common good of the Church." Twenty years later, in 1858, he wrote these lines to Dom Pitra: "Despite all the tremors, Solesmes has prospered and will prosper. As weak as it is, this monastery is helpful to the Holy See, and it can be said, without danger of the sin of pride, that were it to cease to exist, the Roman doctrines would lose some adherents in France. All enemies of Rome detest it and all friends lavish it with honor and affection."

Dom Guéranger's attachment to the head of the Church would suggest that he longed to be at the pontiff's feet as often as possible. But his four trips to Rome did not bear this out; they were made solely to set straight the problems of Solesmes—securing approbation of the constitutions in 1837 and of the Congregation's Proper in 1856, and obtaining acknowledgment of the independence of the abbey's Regulars in 1843 and 1851.

To Gregory XVI, whom he saw only three times, he owed the Benedictine renewal in France; but he regretted the timidity of the old Camaldese toward European governments. The advent of Pius IX in 1846 gave him hope. He didn't know Monsignor Mastaï-Ferretti, but the new pope soon heard about the abbot of Solesmes. When the latter came to Rome in November 1851, he was hailed as a *"gran liturgista"* and was granted five audiences in three months. But even adding the two interviews of 1856, these two servants of the Church met relatively few times. Notes of their conversations, which can be found in Dom Guéranger's diary, demonstrate a refreshing freedom of thought. The Pope, "very affable and gentle, less imposing than Gregory XVI," is relaxed, jovial even, at peace in soul despite his cares. As for the monk, his respectful attitude stems from the simplicity and frankness of a man who has nothing to hide. Naturally, Solesmes's affairs are spoken of, as are events in France and Italy. Pius IX speaks of his fears for monasticism on the peninsula and of the hope he places on the French monks. The abbot, for his part, presents the Pope with the latest works of his monastery and the requests of his friends—the approbation of the French custom of communing at Midnight Mass and extending the feast of the Sacred Heart. Also discussed is a secret work, a work concerning the proclamation of the dogma of the Immaculate Conception.

This schema, *Quemadmodum Ecclesiae*—not to be confused with the *Memoir on the Immaculate Conception*, published in 1850—was never intended to be anything but a rough draft. The abbot of Solesmes worked on it in January 1852 and was told to add a second part involving modern errors. He obeyed, but not without having conveyed to Pius IX his uneasiness at tying these two documents together; and, in the end, his counsel prevailed.

Somewhat brief, Dom Guéranger's schema is a remarkable document. "It represents," writes Dom Frénaud, theologian and prior of Solesmes (1964-69), "the work of a contemplative monk, familiar with Holy Scripture and the patristic texts, who has meditated at length in the light of faith on the great events of the Church's history, and even more so on the prayers of the liturgy." Dom Guéranger starts with a simple certification of the Church's faith, expressed above all in the liturgy. He then clarifies scriptural and patristic arguments in the light of that whole and ongoing faith. As it happened, Pius IX did not use this document word for word, but he retained its general order as well as its liturgical argument.

On December 5, 1851, Dom Guéranger learned of his nomination as consultant to the Congregation of the Index. One week later, he was a consultant to the Congregation of Rites. His immediate reaction was to try to redirect the honor to include his whole community. It seemed, he later discovered, that he had been the object of a *caprizio d'amore* on the part of Pius IX, who even considered having him close at hand.

In the autumn of 1855, the Pope thought of elevating him to the cardinalate. Arriving in Rome the following spring, Dom Guéranger heard the rumor, and it worried him: Pius IX's unexpected choices were well known. But the protest of some of the monks against their abbot in the matter of the liturgy came just in time to sour the Holy See. "You may never know," Dom Guéranger wrote to his friends, "the happiness one experiences in not being a cardinal; I think I would be bored to death by it—the etiquette, the annoyances, and above all the exile. The good Lord has done well, as has our Holy Father the Pope. I very much like this excellent Pius IX, but I like him better from afar than up close. All the apparent indications of Providence, my role—if I have one—everything, wants me in France and at Solesmes."

Dom Guéranger's simple tastes, his frail health, his dislike of official ceremonies, his love of the cloister all attest to his sincerity. He only regretted the malicious gossip suggesting that Dom Pitra's promotion to the cardinalate indicated papal displeasure with his abbot—the exact opposite of the truth.

Later that same year, 1855, when Dom Guéranger learned of the efforts of his friend Adolphe Segrétain to make him the first bishop of Laval, his reaction was equally unfavorable—

as before, it stemmed from his dedication to his monastic vocation. Aside from feeling unfit for the administrative tasks, he believed that his mission was to remain a religious, "a living witness to the universal jurisdiction of the successor of St. Peter," and that his monastic congregation would be imperiled without him.

It has been insinuated from time to time that following his 1856 trip, Dom Guéranger, secretly embittered by Pius IX's treatment, chose not to appear at the Vatican Council. The accusation is serious enough to examine.

Dom Guéranger was undeniably disappointed that only two-thirds of the liturgical pieces he had proposed for the Proper of Solesmes—the special part of the liturgy that deals with a particular saint of a diocese, an order, a congregation— had been approved. But his devotion to the head of the Church was in no way affected by the decision. Any worries the Pope might have had about the monk were totally dispelled by two conversations during which the abbot's erudition, frankness, and dedication charmed him anew. As for Dom Guéranger, while valuing Pius IX's own simplicity in greatness, he always saw the office rather than the person; that is, through his faith, he saw the Vicar of Christ rather than Pius IX. Still, as a stranger to the subtleties of diplomacy, what the Italian thought of as finesse, the abbot considered a sort of weakness. Moreover, he believed that the great pope, and above all his entourage, had little knowledge of monastic traditions.

Was Pius IX even aware of the hostility of some members of the Curia toward the religious? Certainly the monasteries felt it—enough, in any case, to call on the abbot of Solesmes to defend their cause at the Council. Rome, it seemed, had too readily accepted the grievances of a rebel monk who had accused his abbot of having advised against payment of

Peter's pence. In measured, but somewhat indignant terms, Dom Guéranger told Cardinal Pitra that he regretted seeing the best supporters of the Roman cause disparaged. There was absolutely no vanity in these remarks, only concern for the Church—whose enemies were not unaware of the real supporters.

"Instances of the weakness of the Church are rare," wrote Dom Guéranger, "but history records them, and it is not in the interest of the Church's sons to dissemble about them, knowing that what assured infallibility of the faith to the Roman pontiffs in their teaching in no way guaranteed them against any mistake in the exercise of the supreme government." The author of these lines can hardly be accused of adulation; his fidelity to the Church has its roots in faith; it has nothing to do with sentimentality. "Do what they will," he added, "I shall always be in the first row of the defenders of principles, although with no illusion at all about the persons"—a strong statement, and typical of Dom Guéranger.

But the heart reveals itself in action more than in words. In 1858, Dom Guéranger made one of his most difficult sacrifices for the Church: he allowed Dom Pitra to leave for Rome. The cardinalate of this son five years later somewhat repaid the generosity of the father, but nothing could compensate for the separation of the two men.

Toward the close of 1859, Pius IX asked Dom Guéranger to write a secret report on contemporary thought, a work that would be used for the Syllabus of 1864. The Pope would like to have seen his dear abbot again, and did not hesitate to let him know it, if indirectly, but Dom Guéranger was prevented from acquiescing by the foundations of Marseille and Sainte-Cécile, the collapse of his health in 1865, and financial difficulties.

Meanwhile, the Pope—as well as the entire Christian

world—was deeply disturbed because the Kingdom of Italy was increasingly challenging the papacy in its determination to swallow up the papal states. If Dom Guéranger didn't put pen to paper in defense of this cause, it was only because many others were doing so. But he alluded to it whenever possible and consecrated an article to the heroes of Castelfidardo. Solesmes itself supported the papal zouaves— the international corps of volunteers who swelled the thin pontifical army—and all were deeply moved when the abbey's young lay organist departed as a volunteer.

When, on December 11, 1866, French troops provisionally evacuated Rome, Catholics wondered what would become of Pius IX's invitation to the bishops of the world to participate in the beatification of the Japanese martyrs and to celebrate the eighteenth centennial of the Apostles, set for June 1867. "There is in Catholic hearts," wrote Dom Guéranger to Cardinal Pitra, "a supernatural confidence that outweighs the terrors. I am waiting to see something beneficial happen to the Church, something that will confound the plans of her enemies. No one has the answer. But whether by a miracle, or by secondary causes, God will intervene."

At the time, it was thought that Pius IX would use this episcopal gathering to hold a sort of council outside canonical formalities. Dom Guéranger encouraged Monsignor Pie to uphold the Pope no matter what ensued. Their faith in the Holy Spirit, propriety, and even the bishops' own interests demanded it. "The solidity and strength of the episcopate are in their being Apostolic," he said.

But as it happened, the meeting of 1867 stopped abruptly, and everyone began to prepare for what was to be the Vatican Council. The great event, the first council since Trent three hundred years before, gave rise to numerous rumors about revolutionary plots in the Church and around Rome. Dom

Guéranger did not wish to play the prophet, but he exhorted his friends to keep the faith: "If the Council is held," he wrote, "I predict certain agitations; but one must also rest assured that the Holy Spirit will direct all, and that truth will govern all questions. I cannot believe that the Holy Father would delude himself by taking so great a decision."

The participation at the council of the abbots of monasteries met with difficulties, but many French bishops made sure that the abbot of Solesmes was included. Pius IX, who in 1866 had honored him with the *cappa magna* (the long ceremonial train of the bishops) also wished him there at the secret request of the bishop of Le Mans. While not wanting to appear a privileged person, Dom Guéranger began to prepare for the trip, but at the last moment he had to give it up for reasons of health. This greatly disappointed his friends, but their distress was dispelled in January 1870 when the *Pontifical Monarchy* appeared. From his cell, this monk had diffused more light than he could possibly have done had he gone to Rome. Pius IX recognized its benefit to the Church by issuing a Brief.

On the 18th of July of this crucial year, at the close of what Dom Guéranger called "the greatest event of the century," the dogma of papal infallibility was proclaimed in the Vatican basilica. The news of it reached Solesmes the evening of the next day, during the *conférence spirituelle*. The Te Deum was sung before Compline, rockets were fired, and the bells pealed for an hour. A solemn ceremony took place on Sunday the 24th, and Dom Guéranger wrote a description of it in his journal, which is reproduced among the illustrations of this chapter.

The imposing effigy of the Prince of the Apostles was moved to the back of the nave of the abbey church where to this day it greets visitors to Saint-Pierre de Solesmes. The pedestal's inscription seems to sum up Dom Guéranger's faith: "Contemplate the God Word, the rock (= pierre, Peter = Pierre) divinely hewn in gold. Established thereon, I am unshakable." It echoes what he liked to say over and over again to his friends: "St. Peter lives in Pius IX, and Jesus Christ lives in St. Peter."

Rome, Catholicism's center, captured Dom Guéranger's heart. In its eighteen centuries of existence, the Eternal City synthesized for him the whole history of the Church: "The annals of Rome are the key to the ages," he said. It was the unified vision of the man who returns to the source, and who discovers therein the truth by which he lives.

This past he found in the churches where he loved to pray and celebrate the Mass. After St. Peter, he loved St. Mary Major and St. Cecilia. But the most intriguing past lay hidden beneath the earth. The history of the first centuries included heroism as well as Christian penetration into all classes of society, incidentally refuting the contention that Christianity was only a religion of slaves. The nineteenth century saw the discovery of subterranean Rome, and the retracing of ancient history.

In 1837 Dom Guéranger only had a glimpse of this mysterious world. It was not until 1843 that Father Marchi introduced him to Christian archeology. But his greatest discovery came on December 2, 1851, when he met the young Giovanni Baptista de Rossi, who was then just beginning his brilliant career. Soon, a great friendship sprang up between these two men, both of whom were seeking to serve the Church by unveiling her primitive glories.

Dom Guéranger was constantly prodding his friend who, though young and successful, was subject to chronic depression. Without the long letters from Solesmes, which gave Rossi "many days of serenity and enthusiasm," he might never have produced his thick volumes, the *Roma Sotterana*. Their correspondence shows a little-known Dom Guéranger, someone who though impatient with the progress of the excavations, which fascinated him, found the time to address Rossi's personal problems. Rossi, in turn, had these beautiful words to say about the abbot: "He was for me that which St. Phillip Neri was for Baronius." The archeologist came to Solesmes in 1856 and 1865, and their conversations lasted from morning to night.

In Rome, the excitement of the two when walking across the Roman campania or in the newly unearthed passages of the catacombs must have been palpable. The discovery in 1854 of the crypt of the popes, then that of Saint Cecilia right next to it, impelled Dom Guéranger to return to Rome. Pius IX, "the new Damasius," who had visited the catacombs, asked him to celebrate the first subterranean Mass facing the spot where the body of the martyr had rested. April 26, 1856, was one of the greatest days in Dom Guéranger's life.

After Rome, the abbot of Solesmes liked to visit those places where St. Benedict had trod. He had seen Subiaco at the beginning of his abbatiate, and now, twenty years later, he made a pilgrimage (March 30-April 4, 1856) to Monte Cassino—a unique pilgrimage because of the fraternal welcome of the community, the unforgettable panorama of the Campania, the visit to the spots where so many of the deeds recounted by St. Gregory had taken place, and the riches of the library. The immense abbey, at that time, however, had no more than twenty fathers and fourteen lay brothers. It was heartbreaking. Calling to mind the past, Dom Guéranger pondered the destiny of this, the house of the patriarch of monks.

He was all the more attached to the monastery because the novice master of Monte Cassino was a Solesmesnian, Dom Camille Leduc, who, for reasons of health, had had to go to

Italy in 1850. His letters to Dom Guéranger spoke of his efforts to obliterate the worldly habits of the young monks which they had acquired during the days of revolutionary secularism—a difficult task. Fortunately, many of the Italian monks understood the value of the French monastic renewal. Dom Guéranger would have loved to help them, especially since the abbot of Monte Cassino had supported him in 1840 in his battle for the rights of his abbey against the claims of the bishop of Le Mans. But he did it discretely, not wanting to use himself as an example, nor to interfere in the affairs of others.

His fourth and last visit to Rome, during which he visited the Appian Way and Monte Cassino, was "more delicious than the three others," Dom Guéranger confided to Rossi. "The best of my soul is in Rome." Solesmes was, of course, his place of choice. But Rome took him back to the origins of the Church, and through its archeological vestiges, he rediscovered the heroic Christianity of apostolic times. Italy, already ennobled by its luminosity and cultural riches, became a new Holy Land, all the more so as St. Peter's successor gave the Eternal City a sense of the presence of Christ.

Cardinal Pie has captured his friend's ardor for the Roman catacombs, a place where he felt he was in the very heart of the Christian world:

"I can still see him in the catacombs, explaining the symbolism of the different fish with such fire, such richness of expression; he was completely taken by it. And, as I seemed a little distracted to him, he kept insisting on pointing out the importance of his subject until I finally said to him: 'Ah! my dear Father, I have no need of all these fish. I have you, you, and that suffices. You are of the same species. You dive into this water, it is above you, below you, around you, all about you.' It was, in fact, in this precise way that he moved through things divine."

VI

LITURGICAL LIFE

"PRAYER IS MAN'S RICHEST BOON." The General Preface of *The Liturgical Year* opens with the simple affirmation of this intangible truth. "One is struck by its range and religious strength," writes Dom Capelle of the book. "From the first words, one enters into the very center of truth, from which everything radiates. This admirable page demonstrates with majestic ease the primary place of the liturgy in Christianity: although necessary, prayer is not possible except through Jesus Christ and the Holy Spirit sent by him; the Holy Spirit resides in the Church, and the unceasing voice of the Church is the liturgy. The golden chain of this reasoning is indestructible. . . ."

Nothing could better convey the fundamental thinking that guided Dom Guéranger throughout his most famous work, the one in which he placed "the best of himself." By temperament Dom Guéranger preferred prayer in its liturgical form: his refined sensibilities responded to signs and symbols, to the chant, to all poetic expressions of the Faith.

Dryness and coldness inhibited him—one of the reasons why Jansenism repelled him.

But one must go beneath the purely human to grasp the core of Dom Guéranger's liturgical thinking, which surfaced as early as 1830 in his first articles and was fleshed out in the Preface to *The Liturgical Year,* as well as in the first pages of the *Liturgical Institutions;* it most probably emanated from his reflections on perusing the Roman Breviary and Missal, that is, from his days with Monseigneur de la Myre. At that time, Abbé Guéranger was concentrating on studying the Church's structure, so much so that his theological synthesis—the connection between the mystery of the Church and the mystery of the Incarnation—sprang from the light of the liturgy.

Dom Guéranger grasped that the source of the liturgy was at the very heart of the Trinity: God contemplates himself, loves himself, and praises himself. Liturgical expression, properly understood, supposes the Incarnation. According to the economy of this mystery, invisible realities make themselves known to man by means of visible realities.

Christ, in his great and unique liturgical act—the Sacrifice of the Cross—made all believers participants by virtue of the Holy Spirit. The Church is, quite simply, the gathering together of these members, hierarchically organized. In founding her, Christ transmitted to the Apostles his power to dispense the mysteries, his liturgical power. The Apostles organized rites, because the visible Church needed exterior signs. Thus was born the liturgical tradition.

Dom Guéranger loved the liturgy, not simply for its exterior aspects, but for its dignity as the Church's prayer. And as he habitually envisaged the Church in both of its aspects—as the Bride of Christ and as a society, one and universal—he was able to bring out the true excellence of the liturgy.

As the voice of the Bride, "the Church's prayer is the most agreeable to the ear and heart of God, as well as the most powerful." The aim of *The Liturgical Year* was to make the different accents of this voice heard.

As "prayer on a social level," prayer of the Mystical Body, the liturgy takes precedence over every other form of prayer. It alone expresses and holds together the unity and universality of the Faith, across the development of Tradition, but only as it refers back to the visible representative of Christ, the sole principle of the Church's unity. Subjected to the authority of the Roman Pontiff, it is a symbol of unity and offers a complete guarantee of orthodoxy. Dom Guéranger would illustrate these principles in his *Liturgical Institutions.*

In giving back to his century the profound meaning of liturgical prayer, the abbot of Solesmes fought against two forms of individualism: a personal individualism, by upholding the superiority of ecclesial prayer; and a national or regional individualism, by emphasizing the importance of this unity—never to be confused with uniformity.

Dom Guéranger foresaw the objections—that he was sacrificing the individual to society, drowning out real prayer life in the noise of ceremonies. Thus, at the very beginning of *The Liturgical Year*, he explains that the Church's prayer cannot take a member of the Church away from itself. Analogically, a particular church will not lose its legitimate traditions by associating with the prayer of the universal Church.

Contemplation cannot suffer "from the brilliance and harmony of the chants of liturgical prayer" since the psalms, from which this prayer has been woven, are inspired by the Holy Spirit to express all states of the soul before God. "For the contemplative, liturgical prayer is sometimes the principal offering, and at other times the result of visits with the Lord."

As for the liturgical year, it is "the manifestation of Jesus

Christ and his mysteries in the Church and in the faithful
soul." It makes man live according to the rhythm of the
"mystical seasons," and produces in him an effect in harmony
with each one of the aspects of the Mystery of Salvation. Very
sensitive to the movement of life and the unfolding of life in
history towards its end, Dom Guéranger savored this annual
rite. Through it, he relived the stage of waiting for the
Messiah—the existence of Christ and the Church's origins.
Through it he entered into the company of the Virgin, the
angels and the saints, beloved persons whose relationship
with the Mystery of Christ he enjoyed pointing out, according
to each liturgical season.

To live the liturgical year, he affirms in the General
Preface, is one of the most powerful ways to progress in
understanding the truths of the Faith. He himself experienced
this "renovating power": "The faith of the believer is thus
enlightened more and more each year; the theological *sensus*
is formed within him; prayer leads him to science. Mysteries
continue to be mysteries; but their brightness becomes so
vivid that the mind and heart are enthralled; we begin to
grasp the joy that the eternal sight of these beautiful and
divine realities will give us, since by merely glimpsing them
through the clouds, we are already so charmed."

Finally, and very personally, Dom Guéranger saw in the
liturgy an excellent initiation into Christian poetry, from the
Psalms to the hymnographers and prose writers of the Middle
Ages.

Dom Guéranger looked at the liturgy with a contemplative's eyes. He lived and savored the liturgical year before he
ever began to talk about it, and even before he undertook his
monastic work. This is why, as imprecise as it had to be in the
beginning, the Solesmes project included a liturgical renewal
in France. Abbé Guéranger repeatedly stated that he wished

to found "a house of prayer and studies"; Solesmes was "founded on prayer and on divine praise as its principal goal," he wrote Madame Swetchine. If he did not make it clear that this prayer was mainly the liturgy, it was only because to do so would be superfluous.

The title of the last booklet Dom Guéranger dictated before his death was *The Church, or the Society of Divine Praise*, which sums up his conception of the primacy of the liturgy in monastic life. Since the Church, in its participation in the work of Salvation, is organized to praise God, then the monastery, a community constituted on the model of the Church, should look upon the liturgy as its highest activity and as food for contemplation.

Furthermore, Dom Guéranger recognized the educational potentials of the daily liturgy. In the third volume of his *Liturgical Institutions* he explains the artistic flowering that marked the monasteries of the Middle Ages: "The calm and solitude, holy contemplations, prayerful traditions, and most of all, the daily celebration of the Divine Office maintained in the monasteries an inspired recollection and repose in the midst of which the heart and mind sought to envision the physical representations of an even happier dwelling place."

This expresses the entire existence of a monk, an existence lived out at the gate of heaven, thanks to the liturgy. Dom Guéranger allows us to glimpse the secret of the happiness that never left him: "The conversation of these men was in heaven; each year, day by day, hour by hour, they ran through the cycle of the Christian year; they participated in the development of the mysteries it celebrates, giving their entire soul to each phrase. The chants, the pomp of the ceremonies, so rich and varied, daily fed an enthusiasm that was constantly revived, exempt from fatigue; they anticipated on earth the delectable vision that waited them in glory."

Finally, Dom Guéranger judged the example given to the faithful by the way the liturgy was celebrated in a monastery. For centuries, he recalled in his Preface to the *The Liturgical Year*, the people lived the liturgy. But as time went on, little by little, the liturgy was only celebrated by the monks, who were then considered the "deputies of the Church's social prayer." But then the Revolution destroyed these centers of prayer in France, and it became necessary to recreate them as shining fortresses that would propagate a sense of the liturgy among the faithful and help them to live it. The program was immense; it could not be done overnight, and Dom Guéranger lost no time in starting. On one point, he gained satisfaction from the start; as of July 11, 1833, Solesmes adopted the Roman liturgy, though it was still being shunned by the diocese of Le Mans. By example, through the liturgy, the monastery was proudly preaching the return to unity.

For nearly forty years, Dom Guéranger strove to inculcate in his community the sense of the Church's prayer. He was careful not to mix liturgy with devotional exercises. Though he recommended the Rosary and Way of the Cross, these were to be done individually: the "Month of Mary" took place outside the choir; Benediction of the Blessed Sacrament did not include supplementary hymns and prayers; the monks were not encouraged to join the numerous confraternities of the times. Dom Guéranger feared that these devotions would obfuscate the Divine Office. By the same token, though he loved the solemnity of celebration, he recoiled from super- fluity, from all excess. Processions pleased him the most. Seen frequently at Solesmes, they constituted the usual form of intercession for serious intentions of the Church and the monastery.

The monks were the first to read *The Liturgical Year*, although the work was not especially written for them. They benefited chiefly from an oral liturgical year filled with variety. Dom Guéranger had the knack of alleviating routine and sustaining spirits, and of keeping people from going to the Offices "as though going to a magic lantern show." He insisted that a functioning mind made for a better celebration; all religious sciences, from theology to history and archeology, were to be ultilized for a better understanding of the texts and rites. And all human faculties were to be engaged.

Time after time, the abbot of Solesmes did his best to infuse his sons with his own enthusiasm. "How can anyone remain cold when singing about such things," he would exclaim, as he brought out the beauty of a text. He felt that at least some enthusiasm was necessary to achieve a good celebration. Early on he felt that "the great impressions of the soul were meant to be sung." He went on: "Christians are a singing people who feel things deeply; they cannot be content to recite things; they must sing them. For them, there is no sad life, no prosaic existence. . . ." This concept of joy was felt even more during the season of Easter, the time of the Alleluia. The pages of *The Liturgical Year* beautifully express the mystery and practice of this special time.

At the end of his life, speaking to the young nuns of Sainte Cécile, Dom Guéranger summed up his chief care: "I am a busy man, aged and often not well; but I will not have lost my time if I can succeed in establishing in you one holy passion— an enthusiasm for things divine."

This zeal for the worship of God explains why Dom Guéranger expended such effort to improve the material beauty of the office. They had begun in destitution: the sacristy of the old priory had nothing but empty closets. But soon, one, and then another, and then still another benefactor appeared to witness to his faith in the primacy of the Work of God.

The convents of the Visitation of Nantes and Le Mans gave the first gifts of vestments, sacred vessels, and liturgical books. Next came Madame Swetchine, with gifts as diverse as a monstrance in sculpted wood and yellow curtains, soon transformed into copes, giving the cantors the look of large canaries.

It is impossible to enumerate all the names inscribed in the Golden Book of the sacristy of Solesmes. Suffice it to say that most of the vestments and furnishings of the period were gifts. Reliquaries were given particular attention. These precious relics—of St. Benedict, St. Scholastica, St. Odon de Cluny, and, most especially the Holy Thorn—were placed in pseudo-Gothic casings to be venerated.

Dom Guéranger was very interested in liturgical vestments. He also liked chasubles in the Gothic style, a style he had defended even in Rome, which had ruled against it. He was terribly disappointed when some friends, in all innocence, gave him various beautiful chasubles in cloth of gold, stiff as cardboard, sporting the very "fiddle back" cut he had sharply criticized in his *Liturgical Institutions.*

The paucity of choir books, moreover, was felt as deeply at Solesmes as at many other French monasteries. As a result, the monks could not adopt the monastic rite until Christmas 1846, when they received a gift of them from the Benedictine nuns of the Calvaire d'Angers. Finally, in 1860, Dom Guéranger succeeded in getting the monastic Breviary reprinted.

The question of obtaining books with the chant was much more difficult. The monks became masters in the use of scissors and paste in order to adapt the Roman Gradual and Antiphonary to the monastic rite. When the Proper of 1856 came, "supplemental" manuscripts were added. With their large whole notes, these melodic notebooks witnessed to an heroic age, where ardor transcended lack of material.

The same care was given the chant (which will be taken up in due course) along with ceremonial matters. This last inundated Dom Guéranger in correspondence, because once a renewal of the liturgy was firmly established, practical problems sprang up throughout the country. The abbot of Solesmes responded with erudition, but mostly with common sense. Having conveyed his opinion and spoken of the insufficiency of books, he resorted to reflection: "The principle that dominates all formulated rules is—decorum." This was decidedly not an encouragement to fanciful creativity in the liturgy.

The ceremonies of Solesmes underwent a rocky period at first: the small number of monks and the lack of tradition made, inevitably, for a certain amount of blunders and discordant notes, as well as some discontent. But the monks put all their heart into the task and soon attained a beautiful liturgy.

The abbot's example was the determinant factor here: his attitude in choir was relaxed and riveted on God. But it was at the altar that he seemed principally to impress his contemporaries. Mme Cécile Bruyère sketched a description of it: "In seeing him celebrate at the altar, strangers were awestruck. In spite of his somewhat small size, his majestic attitude and intelligent movements were unforgettable to those who saw him exercise his sacred functions.

"He was born for the altar, born to interpret the liturgy, to make understood the least nuances of its symbols. Never slow, never hestitating, never the wrong notes that disrupt the beauty of the rites. And he, so lively, brought more to it than just patience; by a grave self-possession, he seemed to inspire in all around him this perfect harmony of movement and gesture, performed with an ideal simplicity—an earthly realization of the Beautiful.

"Nominally Christian men would often feel profoundly moved by his performance. The dignity and the grandeur of the sacred rites were understood and these souls recognized that the liturgy of the Church, thus interpreted, was unique in the nobility of its exterior forms."

Although by this time mornings were difficult for him—before long preventing him from attending Matins outside of feastdays—Don Guéranger admitted to losing all sense of fatigue as soon as he touched the altar. "The altar is my support," he said. "God obviously sustains me by it." He even asked to celebrate the conventual Mass during Holy Week in order to take the role of Christ in singing the Passion.

In the course of the ceremonies, his glance took in everything. During a Mass of profession, which promised to be long, he suddenly saw a friend of his from Marseille, Père Timon-David, come into the church. Sure that he was fasting, he leaned over from his throne and asked a monk to conduct the traveler to one of the side altars where he could celebrate his Mass, and then to offer him food.

Once someone said he was surprised that he never saw Dom Guéranger "saying his prayers," totally unaware that long after the end of Compline, while all his monks slept, the abbot would leave his work table, take his lamp, and descend to the church. "With a life devoured as mine is," he confided, "this solitary and tranquil prayer brings refreshement." This adoration, which the Evil One sometimes attempted to disturb, remains hidden in the mystery of God. All that is known is that he took on himself the numerous intentions confided to him, particularly those of his monks, with special care for those who had fallen.

For the rest, it is fairly easy to grasp how Dom Guéranger's soul breathed: the Preface of the *The Liturgical Year* contains several passages relating his experience. In them he speaks of his youth, when he underwent methods of prayer that featured questions and answers. In the Preface to

The Exercises of Saint Gertrude, he merely quoted these lines of Father Faber, the spiritual author of his time with whom he felt a close affinity: "No one can read the writers of the ancient school of St. Benedict without admiring the freedom of spirit that penetrated his soul. The spirit of religion is an easy spirit, a spirit of freedom, and, above all, the lot of the ascetic Benedictines of the old school."

This freedom of spirit, needless to say, has nothing to do with intellectual sloth, and Dom Guéranger made it clear that an effort was always required of the soul. The person, he said, who complacently approaches prayer with a few vague ideas about God should not be surprised "to sweat bullets." He exhorted his monks ceaselessly to deepen their theology, to lay siege to mysteries. Having thus prepared for the beatific vision they would find themselves "less out of their element" upon entering into paradise. Without this work, animated by charity, the Divine Office could not bear the fruits of contemplation.

One day, Dom Guéranger said to the nuns of Sainte Cécile, "The great advantage of monastic life is that one advances in it. The great means of advancing in it are the Divine Office and Holy Communion. Combined with the liturgical spirit, the spirit of prayer is formed, and one easily finds Our Lord." Concerning Dom Guéranger's own soul, little evidence exists of extraordinary manifestations of the mystical life: Dom Guéranger was too discreet about his own interior life to leave any, although he did share the illumination he had received on December 8, 1823. We also know that on numerous occasions he was conscious of receiving an effusion of grace—praying at the Confession of St. Peter of Rome, celebrating Mass on the tomb of St. Cecilia, going into St. Benedict's cell at Monte Cassino. On another occasion, in front of the effigy of the Santo Bambino of the Ara Coeli, which he thought the object of a flamboyant devotion, he suddenly experienced the grace of spiritual infancy and broke into totally uncharacteristic tears.

As regards mystic phenomena, private revelations, or apparitions, he guarded as much against credulity as against skepticism: he took everything into account and reserved judgment. His correspondence makes no allusion to the great Marian apparitions of his century. In 1871 he paid a visit to Louise Lateau, the Belgian stigmatic of Bois d'Haine, but it was at the invitation of a priest of Arras, whom he had come to see for other reasons. He questioned the young girl during the course of her ecstasies and was favorably impressed.

It is difficult to speak of "particular devotions" in respect of a man who lived the liturgy so intensely. Yet certain matters did color his spirituality, and they corresponded to his theological thinking on the mystery of the Incarnation.

Dom Guéranger was drawn to this mystery, he said, because the Love of God for man manifested itself in this more than in any other: thus, his devotion to the Sacred Heart, preferably in its liturgical form; the influence of the Visitation du Mans might well have stemmed from this. Frequent communion, which the abbé Guéranger recommended from the very beginning of his priesthood, was the best way of responding to Christ.

Dom Guéranger believed that contemplation of the Virgin also served to enlighten the Incarnation: to understand better the Mother of God was to have a better understanding of the mystery of Christ. He also loved to use images that patristic tradition suggested to him: Mystic Ladder, Gate of Heaven, and so on. The rose and the twelve stars that decorated his coat of arms were an example of this. Surprisingly, Dom Guéranger wrote very little on Our Lady aside from the beautiful pages which he consecrated to her in *The Liturgical Year*.

The same Christological perspective can be found in his "devotion" to the Sovereign Pontiff. "The dogma of Mary and the dogma of the Roman Pontiff are brothers," he wrote. "Both proceed from the mystery of the Incarnation. A mother was necessary for the Son of God; from the Ascension on, it was necessary to have a vicar on earth." Jansenism and Gallicanism had tried to minimize these aspects of Christianity—all the more reason to draw attention to them.

Dom Guéranger has sometimes been criticized for dwelling too long on the feastdays of saints in *The Liturgical Year*. But he could not proceed, all alone, to reform the Calendar of the Saints, for, in his day, they were too extensively used in the Roman Breviary and Missal. In truth, he spoke of the saints as entirely relative to Christ, as glorified members of his body. From among them, he concentrated on those who had fought for the great causes of the Church: the martyrs of Rome, chiefly St. Cecilia, followed by the champions of the rights of the Holy See, such as Gregory VII, dreaded by the Gallicans.

As for the angels, monastic tradition saw the ideal of the contemplative life in angelic life. Dom Guéranger shared this devotion to the angels, which helped stimulate his desire to see and praise God.

"The Psalter, that's the liturgy's bread." This saying is attributed to Dom Guéranger, and believably so. *The Liturgical Year* is written by a soul impregnated with the feelings of the psalmist. The verses come spontaneously to his lips. According to witnesses, the abbot of Solesmes greeted news of joys or sorrows in much the same way.

While totally familiar with all of Holy Scripture, Dom Guéranger favored the poetic books. The young priest's notebooks are filled with quotes from Isaiah and the Canticle of Canticles. Of all the Fathers of the Church, he preferred St.

Ephrem, because the deacon of Edessa sang his theology in liturgical hymns of great poetic expression.

Other details of the spiritual portrait of Dom Guéranger spring to mind: his predilection for Psalm 102, *Benedic anima mea Domino*—a song of thanksgiving; the *Adoro te*; and the *Ad caenam Agni providi*—the hymn of Easter vespers. During Eastertide, the spirit of the Alleluia never left him: this period of the year was "his" time. As for the Gregorian melodies, he could be heard humming them in his cell for relaxation.

Remarkably, given his life of toil and trouble, the abbot never appeared to be in need of renewing his spiritual forces, or of retiring to solitude outside his monastery. Discouragement and depression seemed to be unknown to him. Sadness and anger (sensed in some letters) could flare up, but only for an instant, and they never showed on his face.

An optimistic temperament hardly explains this. Rather, from the special grace of his position, Dom Guéranger was able to keep his soul at peace and to transmit that peace to those around him. The spiritual counsels in his letters hint at his personal experience. In a letter to one of his monks, who was prone to melancholy, he said: "Try to live with God, without an effort of the head, but as a friend, because his conversation has absolutely no bitterness in it." And to Cécile Bruyère: "Whoever allows himself to be troubled doesn't belong to himself anymore and ceases to hear the interior voice of God."

When in 1843 Montalembert feared for Solesmes, he shouted at his abbot: "I see nothing of that 'Pax' that you proclaim at the heading of all your letters." He had lost sight of the fact that his friend's center of peace was inside himself. "God inhabits peace, and peace is the most delicious gift of the Holy Spirit," the prior had written to Madame Swetchine in 1833.

But the intimate, daily colloquy of the monk with God was fed principally by the Divine Office and the celebration of the holy mysteries, which the general Preface of *The Liturgical Year* tells us is the vital breath of the soul. Without doubt, Dom Guéranger revealed himself completely in these pages. His friends noted how he lived the great feasts of the year: they seemed to bring him rest and renew his strength.

Carried away by "the marvelous waters of the liturgy," as he put it, he knew how to close his ears to the voices that sought to disquiet him, and to shut his eyes to the distractions of events. "One of the great happinesses of our state," he observed one day, "is to let ourselves go with the current, because the liturgical life is a great and mighty river."

The present chapter on liturgy seems the best place to discuss the work accomplished under Dom Guéranger's inspiration in the field of Gregorian chant. It might, of course, have been inserted in the chapter on studies and listed as just one among the many research projects undertaken by the monks of Solesmes. But the chant is so closely tied in with the liturgy and Divine Office that Dom Guéranger himself considered its restoration a sacred duty and the most important of his monks' scholarly endeavors.

In his *Liturgical Institutions*, he insisted that any renewal of liturgical studies had to include a restoration of Gregorian chant. He considered it indispensable to his return to the study of tradition.

Subsequent research has proved how right Dom Guéranger was:

The deepest roots of Gregorian chant stem back to the origins of the Christian Church. The most primitive form of its modality and its earliest recitation tones could very well reflect the liturgy of the ancient Jewish synagogues. But the ornate pieces of the Mass repertory came about after a fairly long evolution. After various stages of development in Rome, they are thought to have received their definitive, classical form in Gaul around the middle of the eighth century, immediately after the introduction of the Roman liturgy into the Frankish Empire under Pepin the Short and the emperor Charlemagne. From there, the repertory was rapidly disseminated throughout Europe in the form of an oral tradition.

The melodies were not written down until the end of the ninth century. The first manuscript notation consisted simply of neumatic designs, without staves, placed above the Latin text. The neums were imprecise about the melodic intervals, serving only as simple reminders to cantors who knew the melody by heart, but they gave very exact indications about the rhythm and interpretation.

As time went on, notation on lines was developed. But when the melodies were transferred to this new form of musical writing, the nuances of the ancient manuscripts were progressively lost, and the meaning of the neums was soon forgotten. By the time a semiofficial printed edition of the Mass repertory was published in Rome after the Council of Trent at the request of the Holy See, the chant had been completely stripped of its rhythmic vitality, and the melodic line itself had become hopelessly distorted. And yet this flawed *Medicean Edition* (named after the Roman printer who published it) was to exercise tremendous authority for almost three centuries.

Dom Guéranger was keenly aware of this terrible state of disrepair. Writing in 1846 he declared that the sixteenth-century Roman editions had "corrupted" the melodies "in an effort to abridge them." They were partly responsible for the fact that the authentic chant was "forgotten, mutilated, changed, altered." Dom Guéranger also knew that many of the independent French editions of Roman chant, despite numerous errors and alterations, "represented the ancient manuscripts a thousand times better" than the vast majority of chant books existing in other parts of the world, which simply reproduced the faulty Italian Renaissance versions.

Moreover, at this period, France was experiencing revived interest in Gregorian chant. One by one, the various French dioceses, thanks in large part to the influence of Dom Guéranger, were abandoning their idiosyncratic "neo-Gallican" liturgies and returning to the unity of the Roman liturgy. Quite naturally they also sought to recover an authentic version of Gregorian chant. Dom Guéranger was bombarded with calls for help. Musicologists and publishers came to him for advice and dedicated their works to him. Although prophets are rarely received in their own home towns, even Bishop Bouvier of Le Mans, frequently at odds with Dom Guéranger, asked Solesmes in 1853 to assist him in bringing the true chant of the Church back to his diocese.

In this field, the abbot of Solesmes was for the most part unable to undertake the work personally. But he earned credit for intuitively laying down the guidelines which others would follow. For a restoration of the primitive melodies, he advocated a return to the medieval manuscripts, the earliest written sources of the chant. He also proposed making comparisons between the oldest and best manuscripts from the different regions. Today, this seems the only sensible method, but at the time the idea was very bold indeed. Many people still considered the ancient manuscripts to be indecipherable, and, in any case, of no interest to the Church. True, a scholar at the Montpellier Medical School library accidentally stumbled upon what might well be called a "Rosetta Stone" manuscript of Gregorian chant in 1847. In this eleventh-century manuscript, originally from Dijon, the neums were accompanied by letters (a, b, c, etc.), clearly indicating the names of the notes. This spectacular discovery definitively opened the way to a vast domain of paleographic investigation.

Still, the practical difficulties must have appeared quite formidable. Solesmes was a small, simple, poorly equipped monastery situated in the country, far from any important library. How was it to undertake all the comparative research necessary for a restoration of the original version of the chant, "the primitive text of St. Gregory," to quote Dom Guéranger's exact words, when he conceived the problem? (Today, of course, no one considers St. Gregory to be the actual composer of the musical repertory that bears his name.)

Well aware of the exacting demands of the task and of his own limitations, the abbot of Solesmes assigned the job to two of his monks who had both previously done fairly extensive work with Gregorian chant. They were Dom Paul Jaussions from Rennes, who entered Solesmes in 1854, and Dom Joseph Pothier, a priest of Saint-Dié, who entered in 1858. Dom Jaussions excelled in copying manuscripts, and his work is the basis of Solesmes's Gregorian Chant Scriptorium, "la Paléo," which was to become famous at the turn of the century.

In those days, the research required continual delving in libraries. At first, Dom Guéranger would borrow manuscripts whenever he went on a trip. Soon, however, the copyists themselves took off on trips in quest of their sources. Dom Pothier's journeys took him east, and on one such trip he stayed at Saint Gall in Switzerland. There, he transcribed onto lines, with stunning accuracy, the famous Codex 359 which was written in pure neums.

But Dom Guéranger had a task of even greater importance to tackle. Before launching his monks into research for a critical restoration of the authentic Gregorian melodies, he wanted to instill in them the musical style appropriate for singing the chant. Better, he thought, to interpret mediocre versions well than to sing authentically restored Gregorian melodies in a manner that distorted their true religious character.

Here Dom Guéranger had only to rely on plain common sense and on his own keen religious and aesthetic instincts. These enabled him to grasp immediately what has proved to be the most essential characteristic of Gregorian rhythm: its strict and complete dependence upon the Latin text, with its proper accentuation. The text contains the words of prayer, drawn most often from the Latin version of Holy Scripture, and more particularly from the Psalms. The melodies were meant to enhance the declamation of the sacred text, highlighting the accents of the Latin words and creating a musical phrase which corresponds perfectly to the literary phrase. In order for this highlighting to come across when the melodies are chanted, the notes grouped together on a syllable or word must be sung in a supple, free-flowing manner.

One of the most serious defects of the chant as it was still being sung in France during the first half of the nineteenth century was the practice of "beating out each note." Each individual note was stressed heavily and drawn out. In the faulty editions of the period, the notes could be printed in three different shapes: simple squares, squares with a stem attached, or lozenges; and various (conflicting) systems had been devised to establish metrical equality or strict proportional time relationships (long notes, and short notes half as long, etc.) between these different categories. These aberrations had been extrapolated from modern music and were entirely foreign to authentic Gregorian aesthetics. Worst of all, the beating of time, and the greatly exaggerated stress given to each note, slowed the flow of the text, fragmenting the words into a series of barely intelligible syllables, and totally distorting the shape of the phrase. Under these circumstances, it became impossible for the chant to serve as an effective vehicle for prayer and meditation. To use the words of the abbot of Solesmes, Gregorian chant had become "a heavy and tedious succession of square notes, incapable of suggesting the least bit of feeling or of saying anything whatsoever to the soul."

Dom Guéranger's big initial step was to banish from Solesmes the practice of beating out the notes. The results were spectacular. Words took on their true meaning, and the musical phrases recovered much of their natural suppleness and beauty. As Dom Pothier wrote, "He [Dom Guéranger] succeeded in giving the Gregorian melodies an accent, a rhythm, that no one seemed to have dreamed possible."

In 1853, just as he was on the verge of setting up a new monastic foundation at Ligugé near Poitiers, Dom Guéranger still felt obliged to apologize to the local bishop, Monsignor Pie, for his monks' singing: "They are really not very good." But ten years later, Canon Gontier, a priest of Le Mans, was speaking in entirely different terms: "I don't believe one could find a better interpretation of plain chant anywhere else.... " A "Solesmes style" had already come into being. True, some observers found the singing overly light. To counter criticism of this kind, and in order to justify the newly recovered free rhythms of Gregorian chant, Canon Gontier went about setting down some basic principles for the proper accentuation of the melody and text. His musical theory was inspired by the new Solesmes performance practices which he sought to explain and justify. In turn, the Solesmes performance practices were the result of Dom Guéranger's fundamental intuitions.

Other factors also contributed to the progress of the chant:

the chant lessons given by Dom Jausions; Dom Guéranger's decision not to allow a choir monk to make profession unless he was capable of singing intonations; and the printing, in 1864, of the *Directorium chori*, a small book intended for the cantors, containing under one cover the "common tones" (that is, the melodies recurring daily as opposed to those proper to a particular feast or season) for both the Mass and the Divine Office. This *Directorium chori* also provided rules for accenting and pronouncing the Latin text. Prepared by Dom Pothier and Dom Jausions, the book was the first product of Solesmes' Gregorian chant restoration. Unfortunately, it was destined never to be used. When it first came off the press, Dom Guéranger hesitated to adopt it, for reasons that are not entirely clear. Perhaps he feared to displease his First Cantor, Dom Fonteinne, who had not had a part in the preparation. Or he may have discerned differences of opinion between the authors themselves. Canon Gontier attempted to overcome Dom Guéranger's hesitancy, but in vain. (All but four copies of the book, the only four still in existence today, were left waiting at the printer's shop and were destroyed when the establishment burned down more than a year later, in 1866).

After this adventure, Canon Gontier begged Solesmes to publish a new *Gradual* (the book containing the complete chant repertory for Mass) at once. Work began immediately, but it took a long time, since the monks could only proceed with the work when not taken up by other conventual tasks. Moreover, Dom Guéranger insisted that problems of interpretation be resolved prior to any printing. At his request, Dom Pothier drew up a kind of "method" for the rhythmic execution of the chant. This work, substantially reproduced under the title, *The Gregorian Melodies*, was not published until 1880, five years after the death of Dom Guéranger, although the abbot had approved Dom Pothier's original text in 1869. In the same year, a first draft of the new *Gradual* was completed, although it was not published until 1883. Work on the *Antiphonary* (the repertory for the Divine Office; i.e., Laudes, Vespers, etc.) and the *Processional* (the chants used for processions) was also well underway.

"And thus," concludes Dom Pierre Combe, author of the authoritative history book on the Gregorian chant restoration at Solesmes, "by the time Dom Guéranger died, the Gregorian restoration was already in possession of its charter or rule book. The basic guiding principles, concerning both practical performance and critical restitutions of the melodies, had been set down by the abbot of Solesmes himself; and the first practical editions of the chant were already being prepared."

Solesmes had not as yet received from Rome the official mission to revise the liturgical chant books of the Universal Church. (This special assignment did not come until the Motu Proprio of Pope Pius X in 1903.) But the beauty of divine worship was at stake, and Dom Guéranger had no qualms whatsoever about starting on his own initiative: the musical patrimony of the Church was at stake; it had to be recovered and then promoted.

VII

STUDIES

AFTER THE CHURCH, NO OTHER PLACE WAS DEARER to Dom Guéranger than his cell. It is there that he received his monks and friends, there that he worked.

Located on the northwest corner of the priory, with a view of the Sarthe on one side and of Sablé on the other, it consisted of two small rooms. In the first was a rustic chest of drawers and a great desk loaded down with books and papers. He lived in the other room, a small bedroom with a bed, three chairs, a prie-dieu, a lectern—also covered with books—and finally the famous little table, his "workbench," on which he wrote the greater part of his works and letters.

Biographical dictionaries, often restricted to the principal dates and writings of a person, have presented Dom Guéranger as a prolific ecclesiastical author without mentioning the impact of his works. Unfortunately, his work is too little known today, perhaps because the subjects treated, their length and general presentation, discourage the superficial or hasty reader.

But before going into the array of the abbot's works, their uniting thread ought to be discussed and understood.

From his youth, Dom Guéranger had a strong inclination for intellectual work; he needed to search out and scrutinize the truth, to formulate it and transmit it to others. His call to the apostolate was accompanied by a heightened awareness of a grave problem: the clergy's terrible lack of intellectual formation. In order to counter the false ideas held by Christians, wouldn't it be wise to begin by educating the teachers?

Abbé Guéranger was convinced that renewal depended on returning to the study of Tradition, to make known its richness and beauty, to observe "the incessant and ever-increasing life of truth in the Church," as he put it. He loved to follow the divinely revealed truth down through the centuries, which, though unchanged in its core since apostolic times, had developed through the Church's teaching and practice. Research in this field was particularly efficacious, because to verify "the identity of the Church's present beliefs with those of the primitive Church" was one of the best ways to regain contact with the life-giving sources of faith.

This stemmed neither from a sentimental attachment to the past nor from the romantic appeal of archeology. On many an occasion, Dom Guéranger said that it was useless to look for a revival of the philosophic, literary, or political life of the Middle Ages; the only aspect of those days that could be brought to the present was their spirit of faith. (He was, in fact, far less interested in the Middle Ages than in the first centuries of the Church.)

This great Tradition, moreover, had as its interpreter the infallible Church of Rome; these two realities could neither contradict each other nor be separated. Dom Guéranger found it in the solemn judgments of the great councils, in the teachings of the popes and bishops, in the writings of the

Church Fathers, in the liturgy (a point he spotlighted), and, finally, in "the Church's general conduct throughout the world," because she is infallible.

This, then, was Dom Guéranger's method. It in no way disregarded the speculative method, which he admired on the condition that it be accompanied by what we would today call "positive theology." Historical research, moreover, far from being simply a matter of curiosity or an escape from theological reasoning, was indispensable to understanding the unfolding of God's actions through the life of the Church, and, more generally, in the progress of the world.

"The historical sciences," he wrote in 1859, "are not only necessary for questions of mundane controversy; no one can be a true theologian if he is not familiar with them. In studying the scholastics, which nothing can replace, the theologian must unite science with history whether or not it pertains to the controversy at hand. There can be no complete understanding of Holy Scripture if one does not know the ancient world; there can be no profound knowledge of dogma if one has not studied the Fathers and the Councils. There can be no sufficient understanding of the Church if one has not followed its annals, which are history's, century by century."

In respect of Tradition, history performs an inestimable service for the theologian, and ultimately for the Church. It was thus, Dom Guéranger remarked, that the great scholastic doctors, such as St. Thomas Aquinas—whose *Summa* "sums up the experience of centuries"—employed philosophical reasoning. They did this by "keeping themselves in contact with the Church's superabundant vitality, and thus promoting the constant growth of the primary Truth which first sprouts leaves, then flowers, and finally bears fruit, whose maturity the Church certifies by doctrinal decree."

Dom Guéranger twice assisted in the development of

dogma—or at least in manifesting it to the Church of his time; he did this by working in favor of the dogmas of the Immaculate Conception and pontifical infallibility. It was for him a peaceful task, which he relished far more than controversy. He extricated history from the restrictions of controversy; in like manner, he reminded that the Church, before acting as judge in the controversies, was more intent on developing her teachings, because to enlighten truth was much more important. Here is one of the most beautiful passages of *The Pontifical Monarchy.*

"The definition of a revealed dogma is one of the greatest benefits God can accord his Church. All of the truths which Jesus Christ taught are life and light, and their explicit declaration in the course of centuries each time brings to Christianity a new degree of strength and splendor. The sentiment of faith must therefore cause the faithful to desire development of the Creed, in order to enter more and more into possession of the truth which the Son of God brought to earth. The happiness of heaven will consist in seeing the whole truth; the increasing richness of the *Symbolum* of revealed dogmas joins us ever closer to it here below."

History in service to the truth, and the highest truth; a mere glimpse of this ideal had already captivated Prosper Guéranger in his youth, when he still dreamed of nothing more than apologetics. But little by little, a more contemplative attitude grew in him: a wish to research truth for itself. Meanwhile, he was naturally drawn to Tradition, which led him to demonstrate the truth through history, to convince "by the evidence of the historical facts." As he wrote, "Nothing is more insolent than a fact." He saw truth as being made incarnate in facts, principally in the Church, the major fact of history.

Without a doubt it was through pondering the assertions

of Dom Guéranger on the importance of history and on his care to discover the truth through the documents of Tradition that evoked this eulogy from Blanc de Saint-Bonnet in 1875: "The abbot of Solesmes was certainly called to free history from the formal accusation levied against it by Joseph de Maistre, who had declared that over the last three centuries, it had been nothing more than a plot against truth. How well he brought to the fore the basis of this reformation and this immense rectification!"

Practically speaking, how did Dom Guéranger realize his ideal of studying to serve the Church? Because of the variety of their subjects, presenting his works is not easy, but that is where the answer lies.

Dom Guéranger's first objective in studying Tradition was to offer evidence about the rights of the Holy See. While the monumental work he dreamed of never eventuated, the materials amassed were saved and used in subsequent works and for other occasions.

Elements of it could already be found in his first treatise, *On the Election and Nomination of Bishops*, published in 1831. Five years later the *Origins of the Roman Church* appeared, a large, learned, and austere dissertation on the ancient listings of popes. Monseigneur Duchesne said later that it "powerfully summed up conclusions made up to the beginning of the 19th century." In this book, Volume I, Dom Guéranger sketched his first table of the beginnings of the Roman Church and announced a following volume, which scholars eagerly looked forward to. But the second volume never appeared, at least not in the same form.

Another subject had taken Dom Guéranger's attention, a subject close to his heart, and he did not hesitate to take it up. It dealt with the liturgy, which, as stated, was considered by him the most direct and practical route available to reconnect with Tradition and simultaneously strengthen the sense of the Church among the French people, although at the cost of fighting both Gallicanism and Jansenism.

The four articles were published in 1830 under the title: *Considerations of the Catholic Liturgy*, the program that developed ten years later into *Liturgical Institutions*. The first two volumes of this famous work appeared in 1840 and 1841. In the author's mind, they were little more than an historic introduction to a vast liturgical *Summa*, which would consist of a study of the books, symbols, language, and law of the liturgy, and finally, a theological synthesis.

But in tracing the liturgy's history back to its origins, Dom Guéranger could not hold back from dwelling at length on the neo-Gallican liturgies, that is to say, those composed in France from the seventeenth century on. The tone he adopted, and his criticisms of the books used in nearly all of the dioceses, provoked an immediate public protest.

This *"tumultus gallicus"* was fully compensated for by the congratulations he received from numerous members of the episcopacy, including Monseigneur de Bonald, archbishop of Lyon; Monseigneur Gousset, archbishop of Rheims; and Monseigneur Parisis, bishop of Langres. In the ensuing furor, Dom Guéranger was accused of ignoring the venerable character of the French liturgies and of inciting the clergy to rise up against the bishops. In a number of dioceses people worked themselves up to a pitch for or against the Roman liturgy; some priests suffered because they were forced to put their habitual breviaries aside, others because they were not permitted to take up the Breviary of the universal Church.

Dom Guéranger responded to the accusations in 1844; his *Defense of the Liturgical Institutions* was in the form of a deferential letter addressed to Monseigneur d'Astros, archbishop of Rheims, who had launched a formal accusation. The letter was more than two hundred pages long and took up each point in turn. The preceding year, in his *Letter to the Archbishop of Rheims on the Law of the Liturgy*, Dom Guéranger had responded to numerous questions asked by Monseigneur Gousset. The subject was delicate, Rome had not condemned the neo-Gallican liturgies, and the author was subsequently prudent. But he emphasized the distinction between legitimate liturgies, dating prior to the Council of Trent, and those created after, which had never been submitted to Rome.

Monseigneur Fayet, bishop of Orleans, thought he could crush Dom Guéranger in a large satirical book published in 1845. In fact, he did the Roman cause a remarkable favor, because the three Letters in response (1846-1847) elevated the level of the debates and settled the question on the level of principle. These three small works, a total of four hundred pages, stand among the masterpieces of Dom Guéranger.

The first of these responses underlined the dogmatic value of the liturgy, which is not a simple matter of discipline subject to the whim of each bishop. The second treated the liturgy's connections with Tradition. And the third recalled the importance of liturgical unity.

Dom Guéranger's deepest thoughts on the liturgy's authority are contained in these three treatises, and every reader of the *Liturgical Institutions* should bear this in mind and not be discouraged by its length. The discussion was fruitful, too, in that through it Dom Guéranger realized that it was a waste of time to compare liturgies from the point of view of literary or artistic values. The most serious flaw of neo-Gallican writings was that, in ignoring Tradition, they cut themselves off from the authority of Rome, the sole guarantor of their orthodoxy.

Dom Guéranger's attachment to the Roman liturgy was quite simply that "it alone is spotless, free from all error, as the

Church which promulgates it." This infallibility cannot be transferred to another liturgy unless so authorized. "All authority which makes the liturgy one of faith's sources comes from the Church." The new liturgies "substituted a constrained, variable and fallible authority for the unquestionable authority of the Roman See." They, too, could acquire the infallible authority of the Church, but only if they had "confirmation by the Apostolic See."

Far from pretending that everything was perfect in the Roman books of his time, Dom Guéranger envisaged an eventual reform of the Breviary. Completely in line with his principles, he maintained that "this reform would satisfy all the needs of the liturgy. It would be undertaken with sovereign authority, directed by that Spirit which conducts the Roman Pontiffs in matters of faith and general discipline, of which the liturgy is an expression."

"The Church," he wrote further, "in one century as another, is forever the organ of truth, and the purity of its liturgical forms is also completely and divinely guaranteed in our days by the Holy Spirit as it was in the times of St. Celestine."

The *Liturgical Institutions* and the smaller works that complete it are strewn with such assertions, the directing ideal of Dom Guéranger. This should be kept in mind in order to avoid distorting his thought by interpreting certain pages materially, notably in the third volume published in 1851. Although he vigorously defended the liturgical discipline of the day—i.e., the Council of Trent's—and although he apparently foresaw no great changes in the future, Dom Guéranger insisted so much on the infallibility of the Church in the liturgy and on the continuity of Tradition that it would be impossible today to use his writings against any decision by Rome.

Dom Guéranger's confidence extended to the orthodoxy of the Church's liturgical books, but not to their internal organization, which he knew was not perfect. Nor was he too pleased with the manner in which the return to unity was carried out. He had taken great care to point out that unity was not uniformity, that the ideal was to return to what he had dubbed "the French-Roman liturgy"; this entailed using the essentials of the Roman books while conserving the best of the old Gallican and even neo-Gallican liturgies. Indispensable to success was a serious work on the inventory of the sources and study of Tradition.

In practice, the Congregation of Rites preferred to speed up the adoption of the Roman liturgy as it was, without modification; the only thing authorized was the addition of diocesan Propers. Resigned to the inevitable, Dom Guéranger agreed to help the French dioceses in the composition and revision of these Proper texts.

In the autumn of 1841, the abbot of Solesmes published the first volume of *The Liturgical Year*: Advent, preceded by the General Preface. It attracted less attention than the *Liturgical Institutions*, although it is considered to be Dom Guéranger's most famous work.

Considering the number of "meditations," of "retreats," and other works aimed at nourishing the piety of the nineteenth-century faithful, the importance and originality of *The Liturgical Year* stands out. Even today, it remains unequaled in its genre. It is really neither Missal, nor commentary, nor history of the liturgy, nor lives of the saints, but a melange of all these elements. Composed by a monk who had savored the sacred texts and had immersed himself in the unfolding Christian year, it is, as Cardinal Manning wrote, "the fruit of this spirit of prayer and retreat proper to the Benedictines, like a prolonged meditation on the marvelous order of divine worship."

Perhaps its chief attraction is its personal expression. There is nothing dry or systematic here. When Dom Guéranger finds a mystery particularly beautiful, has on hand extra texts on some feast, or venerates some saint in a special way, he quite simply dwells on the subject. His goal is to make that mystery, that feast, or that saint better known and loved. But always the subject relates to its liturgical time. The reader cannot help but be inspired to live the liturgy.

At first glance, the literary style of the work appears to be strongly tainted with Romanticism. But a closer reading shows that the writing reflects the content. Dom Guéranger himself said he spoke "the language of antiquity." Holy Scripture, patristic writings, and the liturgy were so familiar to him that he would unconsciously include both their concrete and metaphoric expressions.

But if *The Liturgical Year* touched hearts, it was due less to its qualities of form than to the richness and substance of its contents. The numerous excerpts from the great Christian authors and the liturgies of both Orient and Occident became in themselves a commentary on the divine mysteries as seen throughout the Christian centuries, a sort of mirror of Tradition. In consequence, the reader of his day learned to pray with the Church—the first step on the road to liturgical renewal.

Dom Guéranger, moreover, managed to teach catechesis from the texts of the succession of feasts; this can be seen particularly in the pages concerning the Paschal season. The theological teaching imparted, stripped of technical jargon, attests to his good judgment concerning controversial questions of the day. Although more spiritual than catechetic, *The Liturgical Year* could only have been written by an extremely erudite man.

It did have two failings, however: it was often impossible

to find in the book stores; and, most importantly, it was in a perpetual state of being unfinished. The abbot of Solesmes was all too evidently not interested in commercial matters; and, besides, he had had bad luck with his first publishers. He did work on several reprints, but none of them, in all fewer then three thousand copies, ever satisfied the demand.

As for its never being quite finished, this brought innumerable complaints, but it witnessed, in its way, to the good the work was achieving. Certain correspondents were touching in their letters: one was saddened when Pentecost arrived (the book, which started with Advent, ended here; it was finished after Dom Guéranger's death by another monk), saying he felt "like someone excommunicated for several months"; another longed for the return of Advent. One woman begs Dom Guéranger "not to leave those who find the nourishment for their love of the Church in the treasures of the liturgy devoid of provisions." Such appeals moved him; but putting together a single volume required a superhuman effort, because he sometimes had to finish it in several weeks. When working on it, Dom Guéranger would become so absorbed that, instead of the office of the day, he would frequently recite the office of the feast he was working on.

It took twenty-five years for him to get to the feast of the Trinity; shortly thereafter, he finished the manuscript. Thus he managed to comment on the major and most important part of the liturgical cycle. Stimulated by what they had already tasted, his readers eagerly received the last volumes, edited after Dom Guéranger's death by his faithful disciple, Dom Fromage. By the end of the nineteenth century, fifty thousand complete sets had been sold, and the demand was even stronger in the first half of the twentieth century.

Dom Delatte reflected on "the work of peace, strength and light" that transpired in the souls of the readers of the book,

which he considered "the most beautiful and efficacious of the
inspirations of the abbot of Solesmes." Can these goods
benefit our own time? Yes, for although the modifications to
the calendar and the liturgical books following Vatican II
cancel part of *The Liturgical Year*, and certain historical exposi-
tions and expressions have become dated, the work remains a
classic. Among other things, its pages on the practice and
mystery of the liturgical seasons are imperishable.

As previously remarked, Dom Guéranger wished to
return as often as possible to the Church's first centuries. In
The History of Saint Cecilia, he went as far back as its Roman
origins. Drafting this book eased his tension during the troubled year of the Revolution of 1848. The Acts of the Roman
Virgin were enriched by a heavily documented chapter on the
veneration and iconography of the saint. But a second edition,
which appeared in 1853, was rendered out-of-date almost
immediately by the discoveries of Rossi. Dom Guéranger,
however, was determined to overhaul the entire work, and he
did so during the War of the Commune in 1870, in the process
easing his sorrow during those sad days. He then agreed to a
suggestion by Firmin-Didot and published his first—and
last—illustrated book in 1874 under the title *Saint Cecilia and
Roman Society*. This huge tome was a rework of the text of 1849
and was preceded by a history of the first two Christian
centuries, a sort of French *Roma sotterana*—the popular and
best work of Rossi which saw five printings by 1880.

From 1856 on, Dom Guéranger changed course and
published long and numerous articles on naturalism, first in
L'Univers, and when it was discontinued in 1860, in *Le Monde*,
which replaced it. The first twenty-six dealt with the book by
Prince Albert de Broglie: *The Church and the Roman Empire in
the Fourth Century*. It was a courteous criticism, but extensive
in order to emphasize the gravity of the subject. Twenty others

dealt with naturalism in philosophy and history.

In respect of these writings, Dom Guéranger's thinking needs to be put in its proper context. He believed that naturalism was the tendency to veil what was too amazing for the nonbeliever to assimilate about Christian truth, and thus hopefully bring him to the Faith. For example, in the pages of Broglie on the calling of St. Anthony, or of Victor Cousin in his famous treatise *On Truth, Beauty and the Good*, Dom Guéranger pointed out the danger of substituting a true, difficult, and living Christianity with a respectable religiosity.

By the mere fact of taking issue with naturalism, Dom Guéranger was accused of falling into excessive supernaturalism and confusing faith with reason. From their accusations, it would seem that his critics had not bothered to read his articles carefully. Monseigneur Pie came to his defense by declaring that the abbot of Solesmes had clearly distinguished between the two areas, while affirming their harmony, well before the First Vatican Council of 1870. Ironically, Dom Guéranger was accused of disparaging the natural power of reason at the same time as the traditionalists were criticizing him for doing the exact opposite.

Not one to see miracles in every corner, Dom Guéranger rose up against "the secularization of society," the result of naturalism, "the error which is the origin of all those of our own time." Its fruits have more than evidently reached maturity in our time.

Along with his extensive exposé, Dom Guéranger published articles on Father Faber and Madame Swetchine, two great converts whom he had personally known; on St. Louis and the papacy, to wrest this saint from Gallicanism, which claimed him; on Sixtus V and Henri IV, to recall the basis of Christian rights; on Jansenism and its conflict with the Jesuits, and on much more.

In 1858, utilizing an important dossier of the Congregation of Rites, he produced twenty-eight articles—a veritable book—on the writings of Maria d'Agreda. Then, having enunciated the principal doctrines pertaining to private revelations, he retraced the battles launched by the Jansenists and the Gallicans against the *Mystical City*.

He also, of course, wrote articles extolling the Christian archeological work of Rossi and, in 1868, a long critique of M. d'Haussonville, who had rebuked the Church for its pusillanimity in signing the Concordat of 1801.

On questions concerning monasticism in 1846, Dom Guéranger published *Historical Essay of the Abbey of Solesmes*, followed by a detailed description of the statues of the church. Then, in 1862, an *Essay on the Medal of Saint Benedict* was released. It sold out rapidly and was reprinted many times. The same year, he brought out the *Enchiridion benedictinum*, a Latin language compendium containing the Rule, the *Life of Saint Benedict* by St. Gregory, the *Exercises of St. Gertrude*, and the *Speculum monachorum* of Louis de Blois. In 1863 he published the *Exercises of Saint Gertrude* translated into French, accompanied by a Preface which is interesting for what it reveals about Dom Guéranger's spirituality. Finally, in 1866, came the translation of St. Benedict's Rule. As for the *Life of Saint Benedict* that was longed for by his friends, it was worked on for years, but never finished.

Two works are left which are best presented together, for each is relevant to the two dogmas defined by the Church in the nineteenth century. Their aim is to demonstrate that the Church's faith is the major argument in favor of the definability of a truth. *The Memoir on the Immaculate Conception* came out in 1850, the *Pontifical Monarchy* in January of 1870. The first was only a hundred and fifty pages, the second double that size; their relative brevity may have helped to bring out the force of the argument.

The method followed by the *Memoir* is simple: witnesses speak of their faith in the Marian privilege, gleaned from Patristics and then from the liturgy. The dogma of the Immaculate Conception is thus shown to be contained in Tradition and to have developed progressively throughout eighteen centuries.

The method of the *Pontifical Monarchy* is similar to that of the *Memoir*. At first, the fathers of the First Vatican Council had been intimidated by the two huge volumes of Monseigneur Maret, dean of the theological faculty of Paris: *On the General Council and Religious Peace*. In them, the episcopacy and papacy were presented as two antagonistic powers, whose balance could only be attained by holding ecumenical councils every ten years.

Dom Guéranger dispelled this pessimistic view: Gallicanism, he showed, could not "impose on the Church some constitution other than that received from Jesus Christ." After having refuted Maret's thesis, Dom Guéranger broached the possibility of defining pontifical infallibility by placing it in the overall perspective of the Church's doctrinal witness. He demonstrated that the Church had always believed in this privilege, and that the faith of the entire Church at that precise moment was in itself a sufficient argument.

Of all of Dom Guéranger's works, the *Pontifical Monarchy* seemed "the most accomplished, by unanimous acclaim," declared Cardinal Pitra; Monseigneur Pie agreed. The year it appeared, it was reprinted twice and translated into German. Later, Dom Guéranger hoped to rework it in order to make it less controversial and more didactic. But here again, the task was left to his successors.

Dom Guéranger undoubtedly had a great capacity for work. The few extant manuscripts of his works reveal a very ordered progression of thought set down with relatively few corrections.

"It is a terrible thing to write a large work," he once wrote to a friend, "when one can only consecrate scraps of time to it. One never finishes." His community, his guests, as well as his poor health "gnawed away" at his free time forcing him to stay up late. Around eleven at night, when he would become sleepy, he would pour water in his sleeve, and then go back to his writing. Later still, he would descend silently to the church.

When he prepared a work, he would surround himself with books, take numerous notes in notebooks or loose sheets (not slips of paper), and then go through an incubation period while immersing himself in a thousand other occupations; finally he would set to work on the draft, with no deadline.

Dom Guéranger counted on the soundness of his faculties; he knew his memory was good. But he was convinced that prayer was indispensable to anyone who attempted to scrutinize divine truths. He confided to a friend that when he was meditating over his *Memoir on the Immaculate Conception* one day while he was saying his Rosary in the garden, he suddenly saw how to tie his thoughts together on a point that had stumped him for days.

Certain critics have contended that Dom Guéranger's work was overly polemical and lacked scholastic merit, even that it contained "faulty scholarship."

The state of ecclesiastical learning in France after the Revolution was undeniably poor and may have aided Dom Guéranger to win his reputation as the "knowledgeable abbot of Solesmes." But this hardly explains the fulsome praise he received from persons high in the episcopacy and many others who were doctrinally proficient. A few examples are the compliments the *Pontifical Monarchy* received from the scholarly bishop of Bruges, Monseigneur Malou, and from the professors of Louvain. For his part, the archeologist Rossi claimed that Dom Guéranger was the only Frenchman capable of portraying his massive work.

Significantly also, Dom Guéranger's works aroused a lively interest in the two countries commonly believed to be the most intellectually alive in the nineteenth century, Germany and England. Specifically, the *Liturgical Institutions* were appreciated by Goerres and Doelinger, as well as by English universities.

The Ecole des Chartes (the School of Paleography in Paris) made a point early on of obtaining Solesmes's works. Dom Pitra, the epitome of erudition, was another who was awed by the vast number of liturgical books included in the third volume of the *Institutions*. He also sought and received advice from the abbot which helped him in his own scholarly pursuits. In respect of honesty, Dom Guéranger's can be measured by his refusal to reissue, as asked by his publisher in 1858, the first two volumes of the *Liturgical Institutions* because he thought they needed deep revision.

Dom Guéranger at times put his critical sense to one side, but that was so as more readily to reach his contemporaries. "I am but a man of the Church, and in no way a scholar," he once told Dom Pitra. "When I write, it's not for you. I have my public which knows even less about it than I."

The scholarship of the monk was, in fact, limited, and he was the first to admit it. "But," remarks Dom Cabrol, "although it has been possible to point out certain faults in some of his works, they can be attributed to circumstances of the times, to gaps of an imperfect formation more than to a voluntarily adopted system or a particular disposition." The "system" adopted by Dom Guéranger, on the contrary, needed to be emulated: it was to go back to the sources.

Even in his youth he learned to pore over manuscripts and not to take the easy way out. When, in the first volume of his *Liturgical Institutions*, he underscored the importance of the liturgy for the intellectual formation of the clergy, he recommended that its evolution be studied by going back to the originals rather than by dealing with subsequent treatises on it.

He applied this principle to all his studies, whether they concerned history or plainsong. This is why he appreciated the archeological volumes of Rossi, whose sheer size discouraged most Frenchmen. "It is time," he wrote in 1863, "that we acquaint ourselves with the venerable antiquities that connect back to the cradle of our faith, that we approach the sources of the historical studies to which we in France all too rarely return."

This explains why, in the eyes of the abbot, the Solesmes library deserved priority treatment even in hard times. "To give Dom Guéranger full justice," Dom Cabrol comments, "the history of the library must be studied, the library which he created entirely and where he was able to gather together all the great collections, all the important works and the rarest printings of breviaries, missals or other liturgical books... ." In brief, he wanted to have at hand these indispensable documents for the monks' work.

The initial foundation was given six hundred volumes (duplicates) by the Seminary of Le Mans. Orders to Parisian bookstores were subsequently placed, one after another, in seemingly endless succession. By the end of 1833, more than four thousand books had been gathered; in 1857, the number had reached twelve thousand. Many donors added to the treasury of books, ranging from the government of the Second Empire, to organizations such as the Royal Society of the School of Paleography (Ecole de Chartes), private collections, and contemporary authors. The peregrinations of Dom Guéranger and his monks inspired great generosity.

The "folly" of the penniless prior in 1833 is famous: his purchase of the vast collection of the Bollandists. Yet another incident illustrates Dom Guéranger's ardor for fine books. One day, returning on foot from the Chapelle-du-Chêne where the carriage had left him, he arrived carrying on his back a beautiful edition of the *Lives of the Popes* by Anastasius the Librarian; the four tomes were so heavy that when he arrived, after numerous stops, his shoulder had been cut deep by the strap.

To this day, Dom Guéranger retains the reputation of a polemicist. Guéranger ... *Guérroyer* (to wage war): the pun caught on; Dom Pitra even heard it from Pius IX. His first articles in 1830 already showed him to be a "harsh antagonist" and he was undoubtedly cut out for fighting.

But it would be wrong to think that the abbot of Solesmes spent his time doing battle, seeking out occasions of controversy. For in all, he only participated in three great debates: on the liturgy; on naturalism; and on pontifical infallibility. To these can be added two minor disputes: one on the Jesuits; the other on the Concordat. Dom Guéranger did not, for example, enter the fray on the other big questions of the day: the freedom to teach, the classical pagans, the temporal possessions of the Holy See, and so on. He does not bring up these subjects except in his private correspondence. Most remarkable, from 1847 on, he abstains, despite invitations, from reentering the liturgical battle that continued in France for more than twenty years.

In general, he confined himself to strictly religious questions; moreover, he kept from skirmishing on contingent points, never intervening unless principles were at stake and no one else rose up to defend them. Once these two conditions were met, he never hesitated, no matter the personal cost. "It seems to me," he wrote in 1857 to the editor of *L'Ami de la religion*, "that a show must be made against the naturalism that infects so many minds today; for lack of anyone else, I have devoted myself to this. I am such a weak obstacle to stop so general an inclination; but I know that God does not require success of us, and I put forward but one single merit in His sight, that of not being silent while human prudence counsels me to be so."

In certain liberal salons it was fashionable to pretend to be scandalized: how could a Benedictine indulge in polemics when his order's motto was *"pax"* (peace)? But Dom Guéranger knew he would never have real peace if he were to bow before error; on the contrary, his monastic profession gave him the right to intervene: "Doctrine in our country is in a sad state," he wrote in 1857 to an Italian monk, "and it is not wrong for one monk to raise his voice to defend and proclaim the truth, *sicut in diebus antiquis* [as in the old days]." "You will think," he said to Falloux du Coudray (minister of education to whose influence is owed the modification of the state's grip on education, allowing Catholic private high schools), "that I hardly belong to my own century, where all are rather easy-going. This coarseness tastes little of the cowl, but I would reproach myself for being otherwise in the midst of this Babel that surrounds us." And he added, "Today, everybody stirs himself up about persons and no one cares about the truth; such indeed is our illness, and it is that much more dangerous for being unconscious."

The abbot of Solesmes would never be a man of the salon. Being only on the side of Jesus Christ and His Church, he characterized himself as "happy to conquer unpopularity in serving the one and the other." Monseigneur Mermillod was forced one day to compliment him for never having seen him *"aut timore aut laudibus superatus"* (reacting to either fear or flattery). Towards his own friends he was equally imperturbable and frank: "You know that I am one of those friends who doesn't flatter, one of the most difficult," he once said to Monseigneur Pie in congratulating him on his first synodal letter. "Be frank and unconstrained, as is your usual custom," recommended Montalembert in submitting to him one of his manuscripts; the advice was superfluous.

All of this doctrinal intransigence was accompanied by a moderation of form and a respect towards persons. A counselor of the imperial court at Orleans, who had lost his liberalism after conversing with Dom Guéranger, said of him, "I found him very firm on principles, but easy in their applications."

Falloux's comment, on learning of Dom Guéranger's death, are well known: "Dom Guéranger had, among other precious qualities, that of defending his own thoughts or of combatting those of others without alienating himself from his friends." This applied as much to public controversies as to private conversations and correspondence. Dom Guéranger's public replies to Monseigneur Fayet, for example, could hardly qualify as polemical. And his criticism of the work of M. d'Haussonville was so courteous that the author thanked him for it. Again, his refutations of the writings of Monseigneur Maret and P. Gratry in 1870 were esteemed for their measured quality and charity.

As for the literary qualities of Dom Guéranger's works, one reason for their success was their order and clarity. He had the ability of making himself understood by the ordinary reader. It is remarkable with what ease the reader can follow one of his historical dissertations or understand the Christian inscriptions in the Roman catacombs.

Although much of the *The Liturgical Year* is full of the embellishments and stylistic traits of the period, this is not so with his other writings. Madame Swetchine characterized the young monk's talent as "free, at ease, productive." Charles Louvet found in the last work of his old friend "a grand and beautiful style which recalls Bossuet." Dom Guéranger does tend to evoke the classic oratorical style, but Veuillot, a good judge in literary matters, said this of the *Pontifical Monarchy*: "The vast and sure learning, its good sense, brevity, clarity is praiseworthy…. As is also his lively and tranquil speech, which knows its ways and the ways of others; this speech which, with a word, shows the adversary wherein he strays and refutes him in his reasoning and beyond his reasoning. As far as I'm concerned, the polemics of Dom Guéranger perfectly exemplify the theory of art—strength without effort."

Back in 1830, Abbé Guéranger had concluded that the regeneration of ecclesiastical studies surpassed the strength of one isolated man. With Lamennais, he had seen what could be produced in the long run by a team—creating a team of scholars was part of the idea of the Benedictine restoration.

But this was not so easy as expected. As early as 1831, to encourage his first companion, he painted a bright picture of a new Saint-Germain-des-Prés on the banks of the Sarthe; but in reality he was less sanguine: "If there is any glory to be gained by the new *Maurini*," he wrote at the time to Montalembert, "it is not for us; we are sacrificed like the gross stones thrown into the foundations of a house." But with effort came hope, which the founder expressed to Bailly de Surcy in January 1833: "We need ten years to acquire a true importance. But if only we can reach that point then the future of scholarship is ours."

Six months later, his self-assurance had waned: "We will first study," he said to a seminary superior, "after which we shall try to be of use to others.... We are absolutely not destined to become important as scholars, not at least for many years to come, when God will have given us the men and the books; besides, we have to give ourselves structure, gather tools for our work, acquire the outward manifestations of our state. All that will absorb us for quite some time."

Fifteen years passed, and Dom Pitra received this response to an enticing research proposition he had submitted to his abbot: "Here, elementary studies are taken up in the hopes of being worth something in ten years; I won't budge from that. . . . Nobody here has your easy facility, your aptitudes and your zest. Many will come one day to know Holy Scripture thoroughly, theology, Church history, canon law, in a word, all that constitutes positive religious studies, without which no one can become a solid Benedictine. Let us therefore keep silence, accomplish humble tasks compatible with our short moments of work, our health, our ordinary aptitudes, our first and imperfect educations; time will prove to be on our side, but until then let us be modest at Solesmes."

Ten years later, Dom Guéranger would have probably felt the same way. In 1836, in a gesture of humility, he refused to claim authorship of the *Origins of the Roman Church* but attributed it to the "members of the community of Solesmes," not one of whom had, in fact, been able to help him. The first publication by a Solesmes monk other than the abbot was Dom Pitra's, issued in 1842. During that year, the community, aware of its shortcomings, had declined to work on the *Patrologia latina*, as proposed by Abbé Migne. Then too, the business of the priory of Paris had taught Dom Guéranger not to count on the efforts of insufficiently formed monks.

The bibliography of the Benedictines of Solesmes in Dom

Guéranger's time contains a preponderance of hagiographic and historic works; Holy Scripture is not listed and Patristics barely represented; theology and canon law rarely appear; the liturgy is found only in practical books; and spiritual readings appear only as translations of works from the Middle Ages or the Classical era. The foundations of the renewal of studies had been laid, but the work itself had yet to begin.

Several names must be cited here: Dom Piolin from Le Mans, author of several volumes of *Gallia christiana,* who, moreover, did research for twenty years in the archives of le Maine to revive the history of his diocese; Dom Paquelin from Rheims, who traveled all the way to Saxony to study the writings of St. Gertrude and St. Mechtilde, in order to prepare a new edition of them, of particular interest to Dom Guéranger; and Dom Jausions, Dom Chamard, Dom Guépin, and many others who worked on biographies and published documents relating to local history and other matters. The martyrs of Poland also attracted Solesmes's attention because of the contact the monastery kept up with various refugees from that country.

Using no pressure, leaving to each monk his choice of subject and presentation, Dom Guéranger encouraged and counseled; he never censored except when needed in regard to orthodox error.

To talk of scholarly science at Solesmes in the nineteenth century is to evoke the name of Dom Pitra. Professor at Autun, the twenty-eight-year-old priest had just publicized the so-called inscription of Pectorius, discovered in that town, when he arrived at Solesmes on August 15, 1840. He was immediately delighted by seeing the *ichtus,* the symbolic fish of the inscription, on Dom Guéranger's chasuble. Throughout his life, he had an inordinate interest in Christian symbolism.

After serving as prior of Saint-Germain de Paris, during

which time he was able to assist Abbé Migne in his monumental *Patrologia*, he embarked, like several of his confrères, on a fund-raising mission. He traveled throughout France as well as England, Belgium, Holland, and the Germanic countries. The hunt for manuscripts quickly took priority over financial matters, though he continued in both pursuits, copying unpublished texts at night.

Dom Pitra had an iron constitution and was able to function with no more than three or four hours sleep a night. He even used to joke about it. In 1849, for example, he was at Middle Hill near the rich library of Baron Thomas Philips. From there he wrote to his abbot, "Every evening, after the table was cleared, the baron had it covered with his rarest manuscripts. It's what we call a dessert of manuscripts. The other day, the kind lord of the manor fell asleep at my side, and woke up at two in the morning to find me on the last round of the dessert: I had devoured it all without a sound."

This work was utilized in the four tomes of the *Spicilegium solesmense*, which came out in 1852-1858 and was succeeded after Dom Guéranger's death by the *Analecta sacra* and *Analecta novissima*—collections that only contained, as a matter of principle, unpublished manuscripts.

Dom Pitra loved his monastic cell; his cross was having to live away from it so frequently. But he found consolation in his affection for his abbot: "Let me be forever exiled, provided that I be the only one!" he wrote to him before crossing the Channel. "Provided that at this price you may be happier with my brothers! It is your own troubles that weigh me down. . ."

But at a time when Dom Pitra might have returned to the fold, he became drawn to Eastern languages. Dom Guéranger consented to his staying in Rome to continue his studies, if somewhat regretfully. In the end, Dom Pitra attracted the attention of Rome by publishing an article on the Canons of the Greek Church. As a result, Pius IX asked him to come to Rome in 1858 to study the canon law of the Eastern Churches, and even sent him to Russia for several months.

The monk's Roman career rapidly escalated. By 1863, Pius IX had created him a cardinal. This allowed the disciple of Dom Guéranger to render Solesmes immense services, as the Pope had fully intended.

Contrary to the general perception, Dom Pitra's new status in no way changed his relationship to his former abbot. The mutual affection of the two religious retained all its warmth; in truth, it seemed to grow stronger when grave problems arose.

The portrait of the cardinal, painted by Lafon in 1875, can be seen in the chapter room of Solesmes. Seated, dressed in his prelate's clothes, this austere and ascetic librarian-savant of the Holy Roman Church contrasts strangely with Dom Guéranger, whose smile brightens the adjoining picture. But, in fact, Cardinal Pitra was not a withered-up scholar hunched in his ivory tower. Pilgrims to Rome who were recommended to him by Dom Guéranger spoke of his devotion and smiling refinement. "To have made his acquaintance," wrote Rossi, "is as dear to me as the discovery of a collection of epigrams by [Pope] Damasus."

But eminence or no, the heart of a monk beat inside this man until his death in 1889. He suffered greatly in the relative isolation of his Roman apartment of St. Callixtus. After being away from Solesmes for twenty years, he wrote, "I will die with nostalgia for the monastery."

Writing to Dom Gardereau after the departure of his "dear great son" for Rome, Dom Guéranger said this in testimony for his friend: "It is an immense sacrifice for this congregation, at the heart of which Dom Pitra will never be replaced. Men of learning who work as easily as he are rare in any time and nonexistent today. And so the good-byes between us were quite sad. To his everlasting credit, however flattering the Holy Father's call may be for him, he did not leave Solesmes without tears and regrets."

"Dom Guéranger never finishes anything he starts!" The abbot of Solesmes frequently heard echoes of this complaint. *The Origins of the Roman Church*, *Les Liturgical Institutions*, and *The Liturgical Year* are unfinished, the *Life of St. Benedict* was only half written, and any number of projected works remained just that: projects.

Perhaps this was due to Dom Guéranger's nature: he loved freedom and did not have Dom Pitra's aptitude for following through fastidiously on research. But there were other reasons, which he passed on to several intimate friends: "Do I write for myself? I have not written the books which I projected. I had to throw myself into the melee when the Church was attacked; once the goal was attained, another war arose before I could develop my full train of thought, so I left what I had been working on. After all, what difference does it make to me that I left my books unfinished, when the Lord has manifested, by the results, that they had accomplished enough!"

"Furthermore" he continued, alluding to his monks, "if they are looking for work at St. Peter's, they can complete all that I began. If they will just follow the plans that are in my writings, they will make good use of their time and serve the Church. Perhaps it was simply in order to trace out the route for them that Our Lord made me begin so many things. . . . But, for the moment, there is absolutely no reason to worry about that, and I speak of the most gifted among the monks; each one can see no farther than the shell he lives in. They absorb what I say to them very respectfully, they are interested while I am speaking, and then, it is over, and they go on with their lives. . . .This is how men are fashioned, and those around me are among the best."

All shibboleths must be dispelled: Dom Guéranger never wished to make his monks "Benedictine scholars" in order to attain the sort of reputation that would reap temporal advantages. Dom Pitra himself hoped "to strike down the absurd prejudice which claimed that one couldn't be Benedictine without being a walking in-folio book."

The then-Prior Guéranger made it clear, back in 1833, that the monks of Solesmes should leave their worktable daily to go down to the garden. "All are not called to make books," he added, "and even the ones who do have this vocation sometimes need to vary their occupations. And working with the land is the most agreeable and monastic of distractions."

The importance of manual labor had yet to be fully appreciated. But Dom Guéranger had a perfect understanding of the hierarchy of values, and to this he directed his energy from the very beginning. For that reason Solesmes became not a new Chesnai, but a "house of prayer," of liturgical prayer.

Dom Guéranger puts it best himself in the Preface to the *Origins of the Roman Church*: "The Benedictine can be learned, but he is a monk before all; he is a man of prayer and religious exercises. The singing of the divine offices, the ministry of the angels, absorbs a considerable part of his free time, and to his studies he devotes only the extra hours which God and obedience have not claimed. Moreover, he must place his work, whatever its object may be, in line with the things which he vowed to God. Mabillon, Martène, Montfaucon, and hundreds of others exemplified what it is to be a scholar better than anyone else in the world. But they rarely left their choir stall. To desert it would have shown that they preferred to be alone with their minds than to be in the company of God."

There we have the principle, solidly put. By contrast, another limit to study did not become apparent to Dom Guéranger until years later: his duty as abbot. This did not inhibit his role as master, transmitting doctrine to his disciples, but rather his function as author, who needed a minimum of peace and quiet. But he accepted this cheerfully: "I am abbot before being author, I, who in opening Solesmes dreamed of finding more free time there than anywhere else."

With only a tiny regret, his joy at having found a new existence for himself shines through—the joy of a father who gives himself completely to his sons.

VIII

FATHER ABBOT

IN THE SPRING OF 1856, Dom Guéranger needed to spend Holy Week in Rome because his business there was dragging on and on. Although Rome had always been close to his heart, he wrote to one of his monks: "I have seen beautiful ceremonies and heard beautiful chants, but my heart is sad. I would much prefer my poor church and my humble ceremonies, which are accompanied by singing which, if not great, is nevertheless that of Saint-Pierre de Solesmes."

From a congenitally joyful man, this nostalgia is striking. Yet it is so strong that it resurfaces five days later: "In the middle of all the pomp of Rome, of its incomparable music, amidst so many thousands of people, my thoughts ever search for Solesmes, with its completely bare walls, its slightly raucous voices, and its solitude."

During preceding trips, he had experienced *mal du pays* (homesickness), but with age and, above all, with the growth of his monastic family, separations had begun to affect him more strongly. Undoubtedly, he still felt his early childhood attachment for the site—the building, and particularly the old church. But now, far more, it was the community of Solesmes—his monks and friends—that filled his heart. In order, therefore, to return sooner, in 1860 he cut short his English trip, even sacrificing a pilgrimage to a place that was dear to him—Canterbury, steeped in the memory of the martyr, Thomas à Becket.

Thus, to really understand what he was like, Dom Guéranger must be seen in his monastery, surrounded by his monks. The impression that is garnered from his first biography—a vast work by Dom Delatte, solidly based on the abbey's archives, but not translated from the French—is that he spent the greater part of his time dealing with exterior problems, that is, problems outside the monastery. Certainly, he gave himself freely to great causes that concerned the Church, but he did so in the context of the monastic day, always giving priority to the celebration of the Divine Office and the supervision of his house. He was known for his availability to serve souls, wherever they were, but he preferred to do so without having to leave Solesmes.

He also kept abreast of the ideas that were current at the time, chiefly through contact with his visitors and his correspondents, and in his wide reading. As for official receptions and meetings, he tried to avoid them; they tired him and bored him—he preferred to hear of them rather than attend himself.

In his eulogy of Dom Guéranger on March 4, 1875, Monseigneur Pie spoke ably of this facet of his life: "You are probably expecting me to present our illustrious abbot in the limelight of public life. Do not be misled. Dom Guéranger will always be remembered as a man of the cloister, and if one wishes to recognize the principal traits of his true character, it is there, at work, that we must consider him."

"They were so accustomed," wrote one of his monks in

turn, "to consider the abbot of Solesmes as the indefatigable warrior for the rights of the Church, that they never thought of him as the fervent monk, the enlightened director of souls, the superior completely devoted to the welfare of his inferiors, who were truly his sons."

Before attempting to make "Father Abbot" come alive among his own, it is necessary to sketch a description of the milieu in which he lived and worked.

To begin with, the exterior of the monastery was different from the one we know today. The priory of 1722 was not yet dwarfed by the massive construction of 1896, and the bell tower, topped in 1731 with a lantern, truly dominated the valley.

The site of the abbey attracted a host of people. The tourist guides of the time painted a romantic picture of it, among other religious foundations: for the Trappists, the forests and moors; for the Chartreux, the deserts; for the Benedictines, "guardians of the light of the intellect," the elevated and uncovered places. An itinerary of 1864 actually portrays Solesmes as a miniature Monte Cassino.

Being very sensitive to beauty, Dom Guéranger reflected on the significance of monastery sites in general: "For the Eastern monks, never was a desert too arid, a stretch of rocks too exposed. The monks of the West, on the contrary, have always loved the points of horizon where God's creation displays its charms and grandeurs with the greatest willingness. They have taken a holy delight in the works of the Almighty who has ordered all these degrees to the end that man, in traversing them, rises up to Him."

As soon as he learned of the viaduct, which would deprive the abbey of its beautiful view of the Château de Sablé, Dom Guéranger saw to it that the railroad structure at least have an elegant outline.

Before the Revolution the priory contained, in theory, some twenty monks. This meant that Dom Guéranger was continually having to enlarge the house. "A Rule such as ours requires a certain deployment of constructions," he said. Even though some building seemed to be going on constantly, at least four of the finished projects need a word or two.

In 1850 came the great tower, built over the foundations of an old pigeon house. It was the cellarer who came up with the idea for this romantic guest house, which offered a view of the entire region. Then in 1858, the building that extended the priory towards the tower and was named the Abbatiale was raised up one story; its garrets contained the most uncomfortable cells, which were reserved for the novices. Five years later, the transformations of the church and the construction of the new choir were started. Finally, in 1869, a series of cells was built downwards from the priory.

Up to the moment of the construction of the great choir, the church retained its original proportions. It had a feature that was unprecedented for the period: the altar was situated in the crossing, and the celebrant faced the nave, with his back turned to the monks who occupied the forty-eight stalls that lined the apse. Dom Guéranger had had it turned around in that way in 1838, wishing to imitate the Confessions of the Roman basilicas; at the same time he prepared a crypt to receive the body of a martyr from Rome, St. Leontius. At the center of the altar rose the great golden crozier decorated with vine branches, holding at its summit, under a little dais in the shape of a bell, the dove made of silver which contained the Blessed Sacrament.

Dom Guéranger would have loved to have left the walls of his old church untouched, but the community's growth demanded the construction eastward of a new and large choir, which vastly lengthened the nave. The resulting disproportion would not shock an admirer of the cathedral of Le Mans, one of which was Dom Guéranger. With the interest in architecture that he always displayed, Dom Guéranger worked on a style and a plan. He asked M. David, an architect from Le Mans, to fashion the new choir in the style of the one at Saint-Serge in Angers, but without its column capitals. At Solesmes, the ceiling tracery springs directly from the columns, as seen in the upper nave (rebuilt during the flamboyant Gothic period). This resulted in an imitation fifteenth-century style, which, if its decorations were somewhat questionable, had a remarkable lightness and harmony. Fortunately, the acoustics were excellent.

On April 4, 1865, his sixtieth birthday, Dom Guéranger consecrated the altar. The number of stalls had been doubled; the little organ and the new sacristy completed the enlargement; the blind arcades of the nave opened up one by one into new chapels and altars offered by friends of the abbey. Back in 1857, a new organ of twenty-five ranks had been placed in the tribune at the back of the nave (an organist was harder to find). Thanks to the generosity of the citizens of Sablé, three bells were inaugurated in 1859; they were replaced in 1896, and today the original bells resound in Sablé and at Notre-Dame-du-Chêne.

The "Saints of Solesmes"—the famous statuary—symbolized for Dom Guéranger the priory's past and the vitality of a particular theology. He was more attached to them than to anything else in the monastery and gave Dom David the task of restoring the mutilated statues. Designers, painters, and photographers of the heroic age were welcomed warmly, and the erudite piled up one hypothesis after another about the mysterious creators of this world of stone.

Scanning his *Description of the Abbatial Church of Solesmes* one can imagine Dom Guéranger leading his guests in front of the Tomb of Our Lord, drawing their attention to Mary Magdalene: "She lives, she gently sighs; her silence stems simultaneously from sadness and from prayer...."

In front of the Dormition of the Virgin, in the north transept, the visitor can open his *Picturesque Traveler's Guide* and read: "The figure of the Virgin is truly admirable and strongly recalls the Attala of Girodet." Dom Guéranger amplifies this sparse description: contemplating the Virgin in the tomb, he ponders the peace and sweetness of her features, and draws from them a meditation on the Assumption; then he sets about explaining the significance of the Marian scenes in the Belle-Chapelle, which fascinated him by their scriptural and patristic allusions, as well as by their symbolism. Yet, as regards the decorative elements, he does not fail to point out the signs of a coming insipid religiosity.

It is difficult to sort out the entanglement of courtyards, small gardens, and hovels—not to mention an old cemetery— that separated the monastery from the village. Commons with colorful names such as *"la Vacherie"* (Cow Place) retained their agricultural purpose. The monks, moreover, owned a small farming enterprise; Dom Guéranger helped, at least in the first years, with the hay-making, harvesting, and gathering of grapes. His diary notes the effects of the weather on the crops both of the abbey and of the region; and he reacts right along with the people in the vicinity. A fire breaks out in the neighborhood, and the abbot interrupts the *conférence spirituelle* and sends his monks to lend a helping hand.

Gradually Dom Guéranger established a small Solesmes domain around the abbey, a long narrow strip between the Sarthe river and the village street. That world of sounds—the work at the marble factory, the calls of the artisans sounding over the background of the waterfall—is completely gone today.

From his very first steps in founding the monastery, Abbé Guéranger knew he should accustom himself to persistent poverty, but he never imagined to what an extent financial troubles would hound him. Why has the memory of the old Solesmes always been associated with such problems?

It is fruitless to make any comparisons with today's foundations. The Benedictines of 1833 undertook their work with no capital whatsoever—what the Maurists had once had was of course irretrievable. "We are poor," maintained Dom Guéranger, "like humble shoots grown from the stump of a mighty tree blown down by the storm." Catholic generosity leaned more towards "works" than towards a monastic institution that was thought to be useless or superfluous.

There was a host of reasons for the pervasive poverty. Postulants were generally without means; not all could afford the annual fee of 500 francs requested during the formation period. The publications of Solesmes brought in very little, because Dom Guéranger did not know how to market his name. The discovery in 1839 of a vein of anthracite, common to the region, in a field of the abbey stirred the imagination of Dom Fonteinne who spent nearly ten years on this enterprise, but it was barely profitable. And more besides.

And so, it was left to the abbot to hold out his hand, to borrow here and there, from the bishop of Le Mans as well as from the inhabitants of the town, but above all from friends, some of whom lived far away, in Brittany or Artois, and whom he had to visit. "It takes 40,000 francs a year to sustain the monastery," wrote Dom Guéranger in 1863, "and our revenues are very short of that. It is my task to lead water to the mill, and this is not without its debilitating effects."

Dom Guéranger had great confidence in his cellarer and first companion in monastic life, a man of unquestionable devotion, but he also understood that his friend's head buzzed with too many projects. The abbot trusted him; moreover he didn't dare remove him from his post. He discretely took care of the IOU notes, and the loan officers finally came to understand that, though perpetually in debt, the abbot's name was all the guarantee needed. In 1874, Mme Cécile Bruyère succeeded delicately in putting some order into the labyrinth of accounts that Dom Guéranger alone was aware of; his reticence stemmed from a sort of modesty and a wish to spare his community from worldly troubles: "I keep all these concerns to myself and speak of them only to God," he confided to Dom Pitra.

Solesmes's style of life was truly poor. Its abbot exemplified it, by his clothing, his furniture, and his daily regime. If the health of one of his sons required outside medical treatment, he allowed him to travel; but he took care of himself at the monastery. He never hesitated to sacrifice himself for the betterment of their life of worship and the enhancement of the library. And he retained his humor throughout: he would make fun of decorum where it affected himself. The cart that he used to go to Sainte-Cécile has become legendary; designed to transport vegetables, it was attached to a donkey, and he would get into it by climbing up over a chair. The heir of the abbots of Cluny would have found great favor in the eyes of St. Bernard!

Few natural resources, maladroit helpers, unfortunate business ventures on the one hand; on the other, a patriarchal faith and an unshakable courage, eliciting the loyalty of friends. This is how the monastery survived economically during the time of Dom Guéranger.

The true wealth of the abbey was, of course, its monastic family, although it grew slowly and irregularly. For statistic buffs, some specific numbers: From 1833 to 1875, out of 186

choir postulants—82 priests, 37 seminarians, and 67 laymen—
105 persevered and took their vows—46 priests, 24 seminarians, and 35 laymen. For the 68 lay brother postulants
(*postulants convers*), the proportion of those professed was
one-third. Of the choir monks, all but a dozen persevered.
Those who left in revolt against their abbot can be counted on
the fingers of one hand.

All the regions of France were represented by the monks,
but chiefly the west—the dioceses of Laval, Angers, and Le
Mans leading the list. Experience taught Dom Guéranger the
art of discerning true vocations. He would, for example,
dissuade candidates who were getting on in age. Out of the
185 postulants, only twenty were over forty years old. The
abbot had no requirements concerning ideas, or intellectual or
artistic background; what he sought was an open, sociable,
and docile spirit, along with a love of solitude.

The monks' correspondence of the day reveals a real
attachment to their religious life and to their abbot. Perhaps
the first generation, over which the young prior had less
influence, profited less from his word and example than those
who followed. At the beginning, and for quite some time,
Dom Guéranger took personal charge of the novitiate, before
putting it in 1856 into the very capable hands of Dom
Couturier. He, in turn, formed various future abbots of the
Congregation of France (later to be renamed Congregations of
Solesmes): Dom Bastide for Ligugé, Dom Gauthey for
Marseille, Dom Guépin for Silos, Dom Pothier for Saint-
Wandrille. At the request of Dom Couturier, Dom Guéranger
wrote the *Rule for the Novitiate*, which was published in 1885
and appeared also under the title of *Notions about Religious
Life*.

From a romantic point of view—which proliferated in that
age—Dom Guéranger's companions may seem a bit dull. Yet

there were a number of somewhat interesting figures—or perhaps their status as being among the first has created this impression.

Various have already been mentioned: Dom Pitra and Dom Piolin, men of libraries, and Dom Fontienne, a colorful personality who was more at ease in the workshops than in his cell. Then there was Dom Courveille, co-founder of the Marists with Father Colin, who entered Solesmes quietly, without revealing his past, hoping to live the hermetic life in a corner of the garden; and Dom Gourbeillon, the uneasy sculptor, who ended up spending ten years in Australia, where he decorated the cathedral of Sydney. Also among the first were Dom Lebannier, child of the soil, a poet living in a state of constant distraction, "a man of the thirteenth century mislaid in the nineteenth," whom Dom Guéranger gratefully used as a hymnographer; Dom Gardereau, dynamic and optimistic, whose martial allure earned him the nickname "*le Capitaine*" (Dom Bouleau, a native of Le Mans, always in a good humor, was dubbed "the best of men"); and Dom Segrétain, for twenty-five years a faithful and discreet prior, who dreaded nothing save "*l'embarras*"—the troublesome predicaments he was plunged into when the abbot was away. And many, many others, whose true monastic personalities are unknown, because they neither wrote nor elicited talk about themselves.

Whenever a monk died—the first, in 1853—Dom Guéranger always spoke about him before the community. One of these eulogies, and one of the most deeply felt, concerned Frère Jean Gilet, the first lay brother to remain at Solesmes, an illiterate whose responses were so luminous when he was questioned during a spiritual conference that Dom Guéranger nicknamed him "John the Theologian."

Dom Guéranger conceived of his duty as abbot no differently than had St. Benedict: the monastery was the "house of God"; and since the house of God, par excellence, is the Church, the monastery is therefore a Church in miniature. And it needs, exactly as does the universal Church, a principle of unity to stimulate and coordinate the efforts of each, and to assure by its teaching, its rule, and its example, a union of minds in conducting the conventual work. The head is none other than Christ, acting in his visible representative, the abbot. The form of the government is pastoral, more precisely, paternal, as suggested by the etymology of the name "abbot"—*abba*, father.

Unity of faith grows thanks to unity of teaching, and that is why Dom Guéranger put such great importance on this aspect of the abbot's function: "The element of monastic growth," he wrote, "is in the word. The monastery is a school, and the spirit which animates everything within its precincts comes from the word of God in all its forms, by the master which the congregation of monks has chosen as guide."

One witness of these daily *conférences* of the first abbot of Solesmes was full of praise: "He had the marvelous gift of rousing the intelligence by interesting it, by stirring it up. Through the conversational method, with no monologue, he knew how to instruct—showing relationships, asking questions to see if he was being followed, using some new turn of phrase to say the most banal things. He had a gift for putting the profound and abstract within everyone's reach. He was merciless in his abjuration of routine; he compelled reflection."

This liveliness was not always infallible: two steps from the lecturer, Dom Couturier would quietly doze away. Dom Guéranger could, and did, sympathize with this sort of physical weakness. What really pained him was lack of interest, the absence of enthusiasm. As he told the abbess of Sainte-Cécile: "Often, when I explain certain things God has given me to pass on, and I see passive or indifferent faces around me, I say to myself: this is really a shame, God only gave me this for them; I know that they would have to read a number of books to find this out and they don't seem to be at all aware of it!"

On the monks' part, as their numbers grew, they almost never dared interrupt their teacher to ask questions. In complaining about this, he would give as an example the insatiable curiosity of the nuns of Sainte-Cécile.

Dom Guéranger taught the Bible—insisting on its literal meaning—St. Benedict's Rule, and the liturgical books. To this curriculum was added the annual unfolding of the liturgical cycles that fed the catechesis, all of it enriched by reflections that grew out of a contemporary event or the reading of a new publication.

From 1859 on, father abbot gave the *conférences* of the annual retreats himself; the notes taken at the time by several monks do not help much in conveying the language, the personality, of Dom Guéranger. But at least they impart the themes of these talks, a priceless gift to us all.

When the monks of Solesmes heard the bishop of Tulle, Monseigneur Berteaud, congratulating them for having as master a *doctor irreprehensibilis*, they probably began to appreciate in earnest the caliber of the teaching that God had sent them. But the most moving tribute that Dom Guéranger received was from one of his friends, Dom Eugène Viaud. This religious, universally admired for holiness, died at the priory of Marseille in 1872. From his deathbed he dictated a letter of farewell to his abbot: "In calling you 'my Father,' I recognize not only my entire dependence on your authority; I recognize also that you are my master in doctrine, because you yourself have no other master than Christ."

As much as his word, Dom Guéranger's conduct evinced his overriding desire to win souls to God, something which he insisted upon: "It is necessary to be the very humble servant of souls; I know nothing but that," he said. "Superiority is really nothing but a question of heart." And on another occasion: "When I shall arrive in heaven, the good Lord will not ask me if I have written any books, but if I have taken care of the souls which he placed in my care." His letters brimmed with similar reflections.

Charity with him took on a nuance of human tenderness that stemmed not only from a naturally sensitive heart, but from a perfect understanding of love for another. Here is how he closes a letter addressed to Dom Bouleau, one of his sons: "Pray continually that I be a good pastor, completely at the disposal of his fold, for love of the sovereign shepherd, but also for love of the sheep themselves." He was never content to pursue a pure theological charity—a cold and platonic stance towards his brothers.

But every loving heart hopes for a response. Dom Guéranger's tact kept him from dwelling on it, but from time to time, his suffering came through. "I appreciate your affection all the more," he says to the same Dom Bouleau, "because the Lord has not always judged it appropriate to allow me a taste of this reciprocity of affection on the part of those for whom I have had the happiness of doing some good."

Leafing through the letters of the first monks of Solesmes it is easy to perceive that Dom Guéranger had to deal with more than one feeble head and mean spirit. But by a continual effort to control his impulsive and vibrant nature, he acquired a patience which became one of his most remarkable traits. Dom Louis David, returning to the monastery after several years in Rome, marveled at this change.

Since his door was always open to everyone, father abbot was continually interrupted; but he gladly sacrificed his own tranquility in order to be completely at the disposal of those who sought him out. "When I am paying attention to a soul," he said, "Our Lord gives me the grace to consider nothing in this world other than it." His understanding of those in trouble led him to go spontaneously to comfort the disturbed soul at his work. Whenever he left his cell, moreover, he would leave a sign telling where he was, to make sure he was available at all times. When he was away from the monastery, the walks and recreations lacked verve, a certain enthusiasm. He had a knack of making those around him laugh, for although, with a mind like his, he enjoyed serious conversation, it was sometimes a real commitment to search out ways to make people enjoy themselves. His nature helped too: "I have received a special grace against gloom," he would admit. "It has never entered my house, and I chase it away everywhere." In short, the monks seemed happy, so much so that some visitors found it all but stunning.

Solesmes as a family. Good wishes for the feastday of Saint-Prosper, an opportunity for Latin versification, Easter greetings, winter evenings singing old popular noels—much loved by Dom Guéranger—all those helped bring out the family note. Charles Saint-Foi, a friend of old Solesmes, recounted the conversation he had in 1842 with Monseigneur Affre:

"How does Dom Guéranger handle his monks?" asks the archbishop of Paris, a little suspiciously.

"Very well. But it would be difficult for him to do otherwise, because there is something very paternal in him. He is respected because of his superiority, and loved because of his character."

"Is he severe?"

"I think he is the most cheerful man in the community. His paternal familiarity with his monks is one of the greatest charms of Solesmes."

To inspire courage, chase away gloominess, or dispel the monotony that stifles the soul, Dom Guéranger had that ineffable instinct of knowing just the right word to say, and just the right bemused tone to use. It is *la rondeur*, literally "roundness," a favorite term of Dom Guéranger and all but impossible to translate; it implies frankness, simplicity, and sincerity, and it was part of his art of gaining souls. He recommended it to other superiors. For example, he reprimanded one of his young monks, Father Louis David, nicknamed "*Bec*" (beak), who gave way to his bad temper, in this way.

"*Bec*! Once again you've been acting like a nag—the head of a goat (*bique*)! Don't ever let this happen again, or your wings will get plucked. You know that I don't like the serpent, and neither do you. So, stop running after him. As you say, I must make a bird of paradise out of you; but you are quite thin: you could almost say you had been eating nothing but lizards. If I can't fatten your body, at least I'd like to make your soul fill out; please help me in this, and follow the diet that I give you, or else, let me say it again, I'll pluck your feathers out! *Bec, Bec, Bec*, stay well, keep well, and think about your father who prays for you. Be obedient, my dear child, that is the only way to gain life. *Adieu*."

Dom Guéranger's manner may be a little less familiar when he addresses the elder monks, but it carries the same affectionate camaraderie. Rarely has "spiritual direction" sacrificed less to the conventional literary view of it. Sufficient proof is found in any number of his letters, as when he tries to rescue Dom Piolin from his native sadness, or to lessen the jeremiads of Dom Pitra, or to infuse courage in the cellarer.

Some needed to be encouraged periodically. As far back as 1831, Dom Guéranger wrote to Dom Fonteinne: "Go back to the source, become again a man like any other, remember that nothing in this world is fitted exactly to our measure, take people as they are, take yourself just as you are. Laugh at your foibles, at your miscalculations, at your oddities, at your despairs, in a word at everything—except at your happiness, for God wishes this happiness, and you would be more guilty than crazy if you yourself were not also to wish it."

Here, in its entirety, is another letter, written in May 29, 1843, which Dom Piolin received while he was the prior of Saint-Germain de Paris. In it, Dom Guéranger is more verbose than usual, but in so being, allows a better look at his spirituality and wisdom:

My dear good father Subprior,

Thank you very much for your letter which gave a detailed account of your interior situation, in which I take a great interest, through both affection and duty. I fear that to look at your weaknesses impresses you too greatly: God is more infinitely merciful and good than you are weak and indigent. Whenever sadness dominates the soul, producing boredom and depression, it is no longer compunction, which is soft, calm, and confident. What is it then? It's a small, slender stalk of self-love combined with the accidents of physical temperament, and nothing else. You must shake this off, and make an effort to be cheerful. There is much courage in gaiety, as in all other things: and it is also for God that we must do this. *Gaudete in Domino semper, iterum dico gaudete* [Rejoice in the Lord always, again I say, rejoice]. When I am at your side once more you shall see what cow heads and what duck beaks we shall accumulate. This black mood must be destroyed at its source, this humor which is not good, neither for this world nor the next.

In your dealings with God, expect nothing from books, but everything from your will, informed and confirmed by grace. Books will come after; they help often, often too they encumber. But it is quite necessary to understand that, in this world, the sky of our relationship with God has, like the other one, its small and great clouds, and at times its storms. God keeps watch in the middle of all that, and although feeble and distraught, our heart does not always leave him. One must live as a child, and remember well, not only is one obliged to go, but remember even more that one cannot go to God except with the measure of grace given to us at the moment. If God wants more, he will give more. Rather, try to live with him, without an effort of the head, but as a friend, because his conversation has no bitterness.

Finally, my good friend, quite convinced that you are in great need of humility and charity, which, in you, are practically one and the same thing, go your way, and don't imagine that you can be perfect in fifteen days. It is a great deal to know oneself; but that's not the half of it. For the rest, two things are required: the love of God, and time.

I fully partake in the vexations which you have been made to suffer. Put yourself above them, but not out of disdain for the persons involved. On the contrary, pray mightily for them, because Our Lord revealed to us a peace against which the persecutions of men can do nothing. It is peace we have, to feel that he loves us, and that we love him a little.

It would be pleasant to be able to linger over a good many of these letters or notes by which Father Abbot was able to rejoin, if only momentarily, his distant sons, such as those who served as alms collectors, whose health constantly preoccupied him. In his communications, he passes along detailed news and shows his close interest in their work; he counts the days before their return, or exults at the thought of going to pay them a visit. In general, Dom Guéranger put everyone to the job of realizing the wish of St. Benedict: "Let no one be saddened in the house of God."

If this patriarchal stance never made a soft old grandfather out of the abbot, being authoritative was not in character, either, as he liked to point out. The way in which he proceeded at Sainte-Cécile, for example—stepping away the moment he felt he had made his point, consulting the nuns when he refined the monastery's Declarations—illustrates "his horror of the arbitrary and the fantastic in matters of government."

"But," continues Mme Cécile Bruyère, "if he, the least meticulous and least defiant spirit in the world, was broad-minded, detail did not escape him, and he lost no opportunity to recall whatever, near or far, concerned principle." Indulgent with those who contradicted him personally, he was severe with those who attacked God. His intransigence of principles is precisely what permitted him to accommodate in practice. When a monk asked for an extension of a holiday visit with his family, the abbot understood, while at the same time pointing out his responsibilities to the abbey.

Dom Guéranger conceived of Benedictine authority as a living thing, as being charged with interpreting the few grand principles of the Rule in order to resolve thousands of practical problems. Its distinct character, he believed, had been altered by excessive legislation, which in turn had paralyzed the development of the religious orders. This is why, at Solesmes, he often preferred that established custom come about through everyday use. As authorization, he referred to the whole of monastic tradition.

"Write only that which has been proved by usage," he wrote to Mother Cécile Bruyère. "In this way one escapes red tape, indecisions, contradictions, these daily reshufflings that erode respect for the written text. The desert fathers did not write their rule before it had been tested by the abundant fruits of holiness.

"St. Benedict was no exception: he left us nothing but the fruit of consummate experience; he spared us his trials and ramblings. Monastic life is a life of traditions, and the hour when one writes the most laws is precisely the one in which one observes them least."

Dom Guéranger has sometimes been criticized for weakness in governing, for bad judgment in his choice of collaborators. He himself, after his Parisian foundation had failed in 1845, admitted as much. He lacked, he said to Montalembert, sufficient knowledge of the men involved; but he pleaded extenuating circumstances: "A monastery is a world unto itself. Men gather there only because of the common vocation which has called them there. Beyond that, one finds all the varieties of the human species, and to preside in such a position and not make mistakes requires being more clever and more holy than I was."

Admittedly, Dom Guéranger had a certain naiveté—which however, contributed to his charm. But it was also in part responsible for some unfortunate decisions, for some illusions which ended in rude awakenings. But before judging, it is best to examine what he had at his disposal. The abbot understood St. Benedict's most fundamental intention—to take account of the weaker ones and not to require immediate tangible results. Instead of acting brusquely with nature and moving before the hour of grace, he would win hearts and orient souls towards the springs of eternal life. This was proof of realism.

In the admirable letter which he addressed on May 5, 1863, to Dom Maur Wolter, the young prior of St. Martin's of Beuron, Dom Guéranger consolidated the body of counsels that summed up his abbatial ideal:

"Take care of your health; you are going to need it, and it doesn't belong to you. Maintain, by all means, the holy freedom of spirit among your religious, and do everything to ensure that they love their present state more than everything else in the world.

"Make sure that you are loved always and in all things. Do not be a father, but a mother to your sons. Imitate the patience of God, and do not expect the fruits of autumn in the spring.

"Make yourself always approachable to all; avoid etiquette and formality. Come as close as you can to the familiarity that you have witnessed at Solesmes.

"Accommodate yourself to all, and do not seek to accommodate others to yourself, because God has not created us all alike, and you are the servant of all, even as is Our Lord Jesus Christ. Take scrupulous care of everyone's health, and do not wait for serious illness to give dispensations from the rules. Establish observances progressively, and do not hesitate to draw back when you have gone too fast. Do not be too troubled about the relationship of your religious with the outer world when they have attained the monastic spirit, and when it has to do with the glory of God and the salvation of souls.

"Remember that the spirit of faith is the sole basis of monastic life.

"Inspire love of the holy Liturgy, which is the center of all Christianity.

"Make sure that the *Acta sanctorum ordinis* are studied with love, as well as the Annals and the particular histories of monasteries. See to it that theology is studied, above all St. Thomas, canon law, and Church history.

"Finally, make the love of the Church and of the Holy See grow in your sons."

When, in 1838, the relic of St. Benedict arrived at Solesmes, it received abbatial honors: a momentous ceremony. By contemplating St. Benedict, the model of all abbots, Dom Guéranger assimilated his principal traits—so well that in sketching the portrait of St. Benedict near the end of his own life, it was in a sense his own portrait that he unintentionally traced. This can be seen in the following description, which though written of St. Benedict, so well demonstrates the strength and tenderness that infused the first abbot of Solesmes:

"In all things he showed himself filled with a gentle gravity, a firm and paternal authority, and it is easy to understand how he must have simultaneously attracted and conquered the hearts of his disciples.

"One sensed a calm about him and a harmony of the soul's faculties. From that came the ability to see correctly at first glance, and the discretion that tempered everything and reconciled the inviolability of the law with human frailty.

"From the depths of this soul, which was governed by grace, flowed forth a good will towards men, which encompassed tenderness and commiseration.

"A humility which penetrated action and accompanied words gives witness in him to the presence of the great God, Who, by the sense He inspires of His own sovereign holiness, keeps in check anything within sinful and fragile man that persists in wanting to rise up and dominate.

"Finally, the sustained habit of contemplation showed him all things in a divine light, so that his plans and actions constantly carried the imprint of a higher direction which everyone sensed and no one could resist."

IX

GUESTS AND FRIENDS

LIKE ST. BENEDICT, Dom Guéranger did not have to leave his monastery often in order to gain souls: the world came to him, sensing in him a man of God. From the very beginning, in 1833, Eugène de la Gournerie considered Solesmes an important center of prayer: "All Christians are going to go there on pilgrimage just as they do to Mount Carmel!" The reality would be more modest, but those who did discover the abbey and its abbot felt they had found a source of peace, and the number of those drawn to "Solesmes and Dom Guéranger"— as they put it—grew constantly.

The abbot's welcome was proverbial. A new arrival found himself treated like an old friend, and old friends felt like part of the family. The vigorous rector of Kerentrech, Fr. Schliebusch, would become emotional whenever he recalled the manner in which he was always greeted: "This is one of Solesmes' children!"

For Dom Guéranger, the guest season meant that his work and correspondence slowed down, or was even suspended.

The guest house registry lists sixty-seven names for 1841. Fifteen years later, the number had doubled; and by 1874 it had reached 370. The opening of the railroad line in 1861 contributed to the influx.

To lodge these visitors, the abbey made use of the famous tower built in 1850 and of several cottages in the area. On this and the provision for meals, it is worth reading the pungent remarks of Louis Veuillot, the publicist; his tirade against Solesmes's peas became a classic. But the guests came for other reasons.

The infusion of the monastery's peaceful atmosphere and the discovery of the liturgy had a profound effect on souls. The monks' singing was not yet a factor: the restoration of Gregorian chant was still in its infancy, and its full impact was yet to come. Solesmes was also loved for the beauty of its setting, the charm of the old church, and the majesty of the sculptures. Cultivated minds were particularly struck by the library; some few even asked to live out their lives with these "knowledgeable and virtuous" men.

But Dom Guéranger only rarely acceded to such requests. Among the pensioners or *"familiers"* he admitted to Solesmes were the abbé de Charnacé, the abbé Ausoure, former pastor of Saint-Philippe du Roule in Paris, and finally Etienne Cartier, former disciple of Lacordaire and future historian of the Solesmes expulsions of 1880; all three were distinguished benefactors of the abbey.

The concept of secular oblates did not appear until 1868. Only a year before his death, Dom Guéranger, at the insistence of Dom Gauthey, sketched out a small rule for oblates. Unlike other such institutions the oblates of Solesmes formed neither a confraternity nor a third order; their link with the abbey was direct, individual, and spiritual. They were simply Christians who, inspired by St. Benedict, wished to live according to the Gospel. Dom Guéranger insisted that they pursue the liturgical life and maintain a strong attachment to the Church.

On several occasions, Dom Guéranger heard confessions and baptized adults. His greatest concern was conversions, about which he was totally discreet, but on occasion an exclamation of joy would escape—as, for example, in his diary for September 20, 1862: "Departure of M. Villiers de l'Isle-Adam. *Gratias Deo super inenarrabili dono ejus!*" (2 Cor. 9:15: Thanks be to God for his extraordinary bounty). He showed particular solicitude for priests who had erred and who, in their distress, had turned to Solesmes.

"Our guests," said Dom Guéranger, "benefit more from this communal life to which I admit them, than from a thousand pieces of advice to which they are elsewhere subjected." Inevitably, the manner of fitting into the monastic family changed over the years. Because of the community's growth, the familiarity remarked on by Montalembert in 1835 could not continue. But the father abbot never lost sight of the fact that his guests should always feel that they had his personal attention.

According to need, his conversations could be comforting, erudite, or diverting. The numerous extant accounts of them give an idea of their variety; herein a few:

Father Timon-David, the celebrated founder of the youth movement in Marseille, remembered that when he was a seminarian at St. Suplice, he had gone to Dom Guéranger looking for arguments to bolster the use of the Roman liturgy: "He won you over in a matter of minutes by his openness, his great frankness, his goodwill, and most of all, by his air of intelligence, whose initial effect was charm."

Alphonse Dantier, whose work on the Maurists endeared him to Dom Guéranger, prized "the urbanity, the charming friendliness that gave such value to an intimate conversation with him. These were accompanied by a sharply discerning mind and a broad range of knowledge that made him the perfect model of the French Benedictine."

On his part, Louis Veuillot wrote, "Knowledgeable and amiable, he is overflowing with kindness, straightforwardness, spontaneity, and information about antiquity." When Veuillot, not without difficulty, persuaded the abbot to sit for the portrait painter and his friend, Jacques-Emile Lafon, he must have enjoyed provoking him and seeing "the two great mischievous blue eyes" of Dom Guéranger glow with all their force for the painter. He did his best to animate the sitter's face so that it would retain its mobility and rich expression.

Other people saw beyond the more brilliant exterior qualities. "The thing that struck me the most about him," declared a young Lazarist, "was his sureness of vision in sounding out hearts. One glance was enough for him to know the people he was dealing with. I will never forget his expressive characteristics, his quick and perceptive eye, his great goodness, his quick mind that could lift up afflicted hearts with a single word." This last is often found in accounts of the abbot. Sometimes the actual words seem to be banal. Presumably, Dom Guéranger intoned them in some special way, or perhaps his warmth gave them a personal meaning.

The chaplain of the Prytanée de La Flèche, who remembers the cordiality with which he was welcomed to the company of professors and students, was principally grateful for his personal encounters with someone who could guide souls with such sensitivity. His gratitude was shared by numerous other priests, such as the future Dom Gréa, and even by prelates, such as Monseigneur Fournier, the bishop of Nantes, who said in recalling his retreat at Solesmes: "I received counsels from his authority and friendship whose practice would suffice to make the greatest of bishops."

For others, Dom Guéranger was merely a simple monk, attentive, as St. Benedict asks, to those who cut no figure. "During my stays," wrote an assistant pastor of Anjou, "I was able to perceive the sweeping charity that was in this great heart. If he was paternal with everyone, he was so, above all, and I experienced it, with the poor, with humble folk."

On this subject, Mme Cécile Bruyère recounted an anecdote with similarities to that of the peasant of the Campagnia who went to lay his problems before St. Benedict. One day, the father abbot was notified that a man from the country wished to speak with him; he went out immediately, only to hear a story about a ghost that repeatedly troubled his loved ones by requesting that a Mass be said. Dom Guéranger invited the good man to attend his own Mass. "But, Monsieur," said the peasant, "a Mass like that would surely be somewhat expensive. . . I don't know if. . ." He was quickly reassured, and first thing the next day the whole family was in church for a Mass celebrated gratis for the intention of the deceased.

With children, Dom Guéranger was always very much at ease. The little oblates of St. Paul Outside the Walls retained a glowing memory of the "abate allegro." Closer to home, the communicants of the parish of Solesmes heard from him every year and even shared a meal with him. On January 31, 1875, newspaper reporters wrote a moving story about the catechism lesson he had given a little girl two days before his death.

The qualities that were noticed by visitors and guests are revealed throughout his correspondence. The letters show him to be frank, perceptive, very sensitive, and with a naive abandon surprising to those who know him only through his learned works. He is continually apologizing for his habitual delay in answering, but never without a good excuse: his health, daily duties, and so on. "I am constant in my friendship," he writes to the chevalier de Rossi ruefully. "I am too often an unreliable correspondent, distracted by a thousand duties, but my heart is not distracted, it is faithful as is yours." Promises of prompt replies always followed, and were never kept.

During his youth and the first years of his monastic life, the abbé Guéranger was loquacious in his letters. But with age and increasing business, he became sober and precise. Someday, his correspondence will be published and show the fertile variety of his mind, the depth of his friendship, and his sense of playfulness.

A quick scan of his letters reveals the abbot's deep attachment to friends. He does not hesitate to express his affection, such as "Love me" or "I hunger greatly to see you." For despite his serenity in the midst of difficulties and his constant cheerfulness, Dom Guéranger was not an insensitive "jovial" person. Separations were always painful for him. His heart was admittedly torn in two by the rupture with Montalembert in 1853, and the wound would reopen every time he heard his old friend's name.

Like all strong personalities, he knew he was a sign of contradiction: "Our Lord," he said one day, "has given me faithful and devoted friends in large measure. True friends have very much prevailed over enemies. Rarely has anyone been neutral towards me."

His capacity for affection extended to his monks, as witness his recommendation to Dom Wolter to be like "a mother" to his charges. This maternalism was extended to his friends. But there was much more.

At the root of his attitude was a charity that made him look upon anyone he encountered as unique in the world— just as each of his monks was irreplaceable in his heart. This conception of charity shows up in one of the counsels that he gave to the prior of the Carmel of Meaux: "I would like from charity towards one's neighbor something a little more personal. God does not exist all alone by himself, and one doesn't totally do right by one's neighbor in loving only God in his creature. It behooves us also to love this creature which Jesus loved and redeemed with his blood, this creature who is our sister and whose company will be one of our joys in heaven. . . . Let us be more naive and more devoted. We will lose nothing by it."

One of Dom Guéranger's most disinterested and discrete forms of charity was the direction of souls. Unfortunately, outside of three correspondences, there are few accounts of this activity, about which he was determinedly regular. He could not see a soul in need without responding in some manner—although he guarded against applying the slightest pressure.

"The abbot of Solesmes," Dom Delatte noted, "believed that each person is a world, each soul is a special creation, and that the duty of the director of conscience was above all an exercise in docility toward the spirit of God." In accord with his very keen sense of psychology, Dom Guéranger hardly ever plunged into long "sermons." He wanted to help the soul detach from itself and turn towards God. Endless reasonings, glances over the shoulder, scrupulous misgivings were all shackles. "What good is it," he asked, "to lose oneself in infinite detail as if virtue were nothing but a holy nuisance?"

He appealed to common sense, to patience without which there is only discouragement. Accept your weaknesses and imperfections, walk slowly, but never stop stretching toward God: "To love God a great deal is what it's all about. How does one love him so much? In loving little by little." He insisted on frequenting the sacrament of the Eucharist, on meditating on the mysteries of the liturgical cycle. His letters to Euphrasie Cosnard, which go back to 1828, are very revealing in this respect.

The spirituality that emerges from these counsels can be expressed in a few words: "simplicity," "suppleness," "joy," "peace," "faith in providence," and above all, "love of God." It is a spirituality of accepting the ordinary day-to-day things. In several ways, it evokes St. Francis de Sales. Dom Guéranger's guests and correspondents were won to God by this combination of smiling kindness and firmness.

Given Dom Guéranger's correspondence—in the thousands—it is difficult to give an overall picture in this limited space. Even breaking it down into large categories—scholarly consultations on the liturgy, history, and theology; instructions concerning manuscripts to be corrected or books to be reviewed; acknowledgments of praise for Solesmes' publications; recommendations to retreatants; postulants' letters; and so much more—a host of names too numerous to list. But missing, with a few exceptions, were the great names in literature, science, arts, and politics; these, in the nineteenth century, would hardly take an interest in a monk who had turned his back on the world in order to devote himself exclusively to the work of the Church.

The first friends of Solesmes have already been mentioned—Montalembert, Lacordaire, Mme Swetchine, Bailly de Surcy, as well as many other generous benefactors. Outstanding among these friends—aside from Montalembert and Rossi—was Monseigneur Pie, with whom he enjoyed close bonds and the respect due a bishop.

Dom Delatte has recounted how, in March 1841, the abbot of Solesmes came to know the vicar of the cathedral of Chartres, who had just finished his enthusiastic reading of the *Liturgical Institutions*. Later, in 1849, Dom Guéranger enumerated the qualities of the abbé Pie to the count de Falloux in respect of the bishopric of Orleans; as it happened, it had been reserved for Abbé Dupanloup. But, in due course, Abbé Pie became the bishop of Poitiers. "Do not thank me," Falloux wrote to Dom Guéranger; "this nomination will help me forgive the other."

The two friends saw one another from this moment on either at Poitiers, or Le Mans, or the Château de la Lande-Chasles near Baugé. The bishop only came to Solesmes three times. While there, they dealt with current doctrinal and disciplinary questions, as well as with problems that were to be brought up by the councils of the province of Bordeaux, or that had to be referred to Rome. Matters concerning the monastery of Ligugé were also discussed.

Dom Guéranger's diary does not speak of these meetings, but his correspondence offers a glimpse of them. It illuminates the shared ideals that inspired the two men, though each had his own definite temperament. The Benedictine encouraged the prelate to speak fearlessly, keeping himself in the background in order that the bishop "take as his model the Hilaries, the Athanasiuses." More prudent, more poised, Monseigneur Pie did not necessarily share, at least at the start, the views of his friend, but they made him reflect. "The first day," said Dom Guéranger with humor, "he beat me completely; the second day, I gave him an energetic riposte; the third, we fell into agreement and he surrendered his weapons."

Contrary to what might be assumed from his outward bearing, Monseigneur Pie "neither dominated nor crushed anyone and seemed to have no other care than to put at ease those to whom he was speaking." The remark was made by Mme Cécile Bruyère, but might as well have come from Dom Guéranger; he understood the bishop's supple intelligence well enough to know he could speak openly to him.

Monseigneur Pie, moreover, was the one who initially came to consult him; on learning of his friend's death he declared: "Father Abbot was my true strength. I was calmed as soon as I had his approval; one hour of discussion with him was often worth more to me than volumes in helping to shape my convictions, to hit upon the exact phrasing of the truth concerning doctrine and events, which he lit up with the light of his genius and his faith." This confidence was reciprocal, to the point where Dom Guéranger said to his monks one day: "If some words have to be pronounced over my tomb, please consult the bishop of Poitiers. No one knows me better than he; he will tell you the truth."

Other members of the French episcopacy were also friendly with the abbot of Solesmes; there were those, as we know, who supported him on the Roman liturgy: Monseigneur Gousset, cardinal archbishop of Reims, who came to Solesmes in 1857; Monseigneur Parisis, diocese of Langres; Monseigneur de Dreux-Brézé, diocese of Moulins; Monseigneur de Villecourt, diocese of La Rochelle; Monseigneur de Salinis, diocese of Amiens; and Monseigneur Gerbet, diocese of Perpignan. Also worth mentioning are: Monseigneur Bertaud, the eloquent and original bishop of Tulle; Monseigneur Doney of Montauban; Monseigneur Fournier of Nantes, and more. In general, those prelates who were formed (as was the abbé Guéranger) by the movement of Lamennais were in accord with the abbot of Solesmes. Others also come to mind, such as Monseigneur Frappel, who held Dom Guéranger in such high esteem that he asked him to support him in his project to found a Catholic university in Angers. As for Monseigneur Fillion, the bishop of Le Mans, whose goodness made Dom Guéranger forget the era of Monseigneur Bouvier, he will be taken up later in connection with the founding of Sainte-Cécile de Solesmes.

In France, as well as abroad, the Benedictine renewal of Solesmes attracted the attention of the religious orders, notably those that backed the cause of the French monks, both in respect of recovering their proper roles inside the Church and of obtaining their freedom vis-à-vis the state. Thus, inadvertently, Dom Guéranger's sphere of influence broadened, while his works contributed to his fame.

While traveling in Rome, Dom Guéranger had established ties with the Benedictines of St. Paul Outside the Walls and of Monte Cassino. Later, in 1849, Dom Casaretto, future founder of the Benedictine congregation of Subiaco, stayed at Solesmes. In France, although Dom Guéranger did not personally know Father Muard, he did enjoy a cordial relationship with his successor, Dom Bernard Moreau, first abbot of La Pierre-qui-Vire. He even attended the dedication of the monastery church in 1871 and expressed his admiration for the work they were doing.

From as far off as the abbeys of Munich and Augsburg in Bavaria, Einsiedeln in Switzerland, and Lambach in Austria, monks came to stay at Solesmes, as did the founders of St. Martin's of Beuron and the brothers Maur and Placid Wolter. Unhappy with the German and Italian forms of monastic life, these two professed monks of St. Paul Outside the Walls had been advised to visit Solesmes. They spent many weeks there, in 1862 and 1863, accompanied by Brother Benedikt Sauter, future abbot of Emmaüs in Prague. From this stemmed the very warm relations that were later extended to the monastery of Maredsous, founded in 1872 by Beuron.

Dom Guéranger was also asked to receive and form novices from Monserrat in Spain and from Brazil, since these countries were suffering persecution. Dom Wimmer, founder in the United States of the American Cassinese congregation, and Dom Salvado and Dom Serra, pioneers of the Benedictine mission of New Nursia in western Australia, kept the abbot of Solesmes abreast of their efforts.

England was particularly interested in Dom Guéranger. For his part, he looked upon "the island of saints" with the eyes of the Church; he had a presentiment that it would return to the fold, and consequently chose this country as a refuge if and when needed. During a fact-finding mission in 1845, Dom Pitra contacted the followers of Pussey, the leader of the Oxford movement, and noted their strong interest in tradition as enunciated in the *Liturgical Institutions*. From that moment on, Solesmes began to receive visits from the Anglican clergy and converts.

Benedictine England was chiefly represented by Dom Laurence Shepherd, a monk of Ampleforth, who in 1855 wished to see personally the author of *The Liturgical Year*: the work was a revelation for him, and he translated and distributed it beyond the Channel. Dom Shepherd was direct and enthusiastic and won Dom Guéranger's affection. He came to consult with him every year, bringing other pilgrims, monks or laity, and never arrived empty-handed. The Benedictine nuns of Stanbrook, whom, at Dom Guéranger's advice, he served as chaplain, loaded him down with chasubles and cushions for the poor French abbey. The Englishman would return home filled with the desire to spread the liturgical spirit of Solesmes in his country.

In September of 1860, Dom Shepherd succeeded in quite a feat: he convinced Dom Guéranger to slip across the Channel *en tenue de clergyman* (dressed as a clergyman) to attend, at Cardinal Manning's side, the dedication of St. Michael's Church at the monastery of Belmont. On that occasion—for the first time since the sixteenth century—English Benedictine abbots would appear publicly in their habits. The abbot of

Solesmes must have rejoiced in this official resurrection of Catholic monasticism. Dom Shepherd organized a grand tour for him that included visiting the nuns of Stanbrook, Cardinal Newman, Father Faber, and more. Dom Guéranger was touched by the welcome he received from numerous unknown admirers, enthusiasts of Gregorian chant or readers of *The Liturgical Year*. But while he waxed enthusiastic at the Gothic cathedrals, he was distressed by the thought that they were still separated from Rome.

Dom Guéranger always rejoiced at the prosperity of any religious Church order. On specific occasions, they turned to him for assistance, for his insights, or for the influence he was thought to exercise in Rome. The French Trappists are one example, notably the abbot of Aiguebelle, Dom Marie-Gabriel, who obtained from him a memorandum that favored the retention of the Cistercian Breviary.

There were others, too: the Dominicans of the province of Lyon, with Father Danzas; the Capuchins of Le Mans and of Angers, with whom he would so often celebrate St. Francis day; the Premonstratesians of Saint-Michel de Frigolet; the Eudists of Redon; the Brothers of St. John de Deo who took care of the monks of Solesmes in Paris and in Dinan; the Carmelites, with Fr. Hermann Cohen, pianist and Jewish convert; St. Julien Eymard, founder of the Fathers of the Blessed Sacrament; Fr. A. Ratisbonne and Father d'Alzon, founder of the Assumptionists, whose attachment to Rome was of the same stamp as Dom Guéranger's; Fr. Basile-Antoine Moreau, founder from Le Mans of the Clercs de Sainte-Croix and of the Marianite Sisters, also very Roman himself; and finally, the Polish founders of the Resurrectionist Fathers, Peter Semenenko and Jerome Kajsiewicks, who, in 1835, stayed at Solesmes (they even considered remaining at the monastery, and later took their inspiration from the Benedictine Rule).

The Society of Jesus ought to be added to this incomplete list. Although certain Maurists had approved the suppression of the Jesuits in the eighteenth century, the latter, rendering good for evil, had sustained the work of Dom Guéranger. As already mentioned, in 1837 Father Roothan recommended it to Gregory XVI who then turned it over to the care of the Provincial of France. Those who still clung politically or ecclesiastically to Gallicanism, were apathetic to both the two great orders.

In contrast, Dom Guéranger lost no occasion to show his esteem of the Society; up until 1859, he asked them each year to send a preacher to give the conventual retreat; he also made a point of visiting their establishments, celebrating St. Ignatius Day in Le Mans or in Angers. His most remarkable public speech was given on July 31, 1858, at Metz, at the time of the installation of the college in the ancient abbey of Saint-Clément. Several months later, in the *Revue de l'Anjou et du Maine*, he published scholarly articles in defense of the Jesuits, who had been accused of being unjust toward the Jansenists. What attracted him to this order was its zeal for the glory of God and the salvation of souls and its absolute devotion to the Church—the same as that of the Benedictines.

Dom Guéranger's correspondence with nuns is less expansive, concerned mainly with spiritual direction. Visitation and Carmel headed the list. La Visitation in Le Mans was very dear to the abbot of Solesmes. Within a short distance of his brother's house, he went there often to celebrate Mass and join in the feast of St. Francis de Sales. The Carmelites of Le Mans also worshipped frequently in the same church with him on the 15th of October; at the time they had a workshop for stained glass, which did work for the abbey. And he maintained a regular spiritual correspondence from 1859 on with Mother Elizabeth of the Cross, prioress of the Carmel in Meaux, the "Carmel of Pius IX," which he visited in 1868.

Most of the Benedictine convents of nuns entered into some sort of relationship with Solesmes, even if only an affiliation of prayer. The closest to Solesmes, the convent at Craon, received Dom Guéranger in 1854, when the foundress, Mme de Cossé-Brissac, was still alive. The house of Mme de Bavoz, which he visited in 1847, made a great impression on Dom Guéranger, and he later wrote the Preface to the biography of this outstanding nun. He also visited the convents of Arras, of Notre-Dame de Jouarre (1868 and 1871), and of Saint-Nicolas de Verneuil (1872). Finally, he assisted Sainte-Croix de Poitiers when it instituted reforms under the aegis of Monseigneur Pie, who confided the care of this prestigious monastery to the abbot of Ligugé.

Among the communities that enjoyed a rapport with Dom Guéranger (and continue to do so today with Solesmes) are the Benedictine nuns of Flavigny, the Trappist nuns of La Coudre, near Laval, and the Sisters of Notre-Dame d'Evron, whom he brought in to run the parish school of Solesmes. Particular mention must be accorded the Congregation of the Servants of the Poor, Benedictine oblates, founded in Angers in 1872 by Dom Camille Leduc, one of his monks. Dom Guéranger's spirituality animated this new member of the Benedictine family, which was devoted to apostolic works, from its birth.

But to return to the "friends" of the abbot of Solesmes. Louis Veuillot, along with Dom Guéranger, was considered an ultramontane, and their names are frequently paired by historians. Veuillot was certainly one of the most celebrated guests of Solesmes; his correspondence speaks enthusiastically of his nine stays there. The first date was in 1842; Dom Guéranger was in Rome at the time, but the enchantment was complete.

"It's just like living inside a Gothic picture!" Veuillot wrote. The abbot most probably shrugged his shoulders; given time, the writer would look upon monastic life somewhat more realistically. Veuillot did not visit again until 1861, followed by one in 1863, again in 1865, and another five brief visits from 1867 to 1874. Between times, the two friends met in Paris, but little remains of their correspondence.

This friendship, which became warmer towards the end of Dom Guéranger's life, is difficult to describe. Certainly, he always liked Veuillot, admired his courage and profound faith, and enjoyed his literary talent. He even invited the polemicist to share—or rather to brighten—the monks' recreation.

But Dom Guéranger never had much use for journalists, who were too overworked to do more than give short shrift to principles and to make do with a superficial handling of subjects. He wanted *L'Univers* to be a truly Catholic newspaper, at the service of the Church, and to this end, on one occasion he called Veuillot, the editor-in-chief, on the carpet. "At the end of one of his harangues," recounts Dom Bérengier, "Veuillot stood up silently, took Dom Guéranger's hand, kissed it, and left without defending himself." The solid doctrine and calm strength of the monk—which he already knew from the numerous articles published in *L'Univers* and *Le Monde*—had subdued him.

Frequently at Veuillot's side at the paper was Melchior du Lac de Montvert, who, though unsuccessful in pursuing the Benedictine life at the priory of Saint-Germain, retained the monastic way of life. He had a deep attachment to Dom Guéranger, and despite the abbot's barrage of complaints about the misprints in *L'Univers*, he never lost his gentleness. At his death in 1872, Veuillot paid homage to this little known Catholic journalist, a marvel of doctrinal strength, broadmindedness, humility, and poverty. "I believe," he wrote to Dom Guéranger, "that du Lac didn't love anyone so much as you."

And there were a host of others: Adolphe Segrétain, former mayor of Laval, admired by Dom Guéranger for his view of history, who came back to the faith in Solesmes; Philippe Guignard, conservator of the library of Dijon, a scholar immersed in researching the liturgy, who willed some of his books to the monastery; Léon Gautier, still a young historian, who included Dom Guéranger in his *Literary Portraits* and said that *The Liturgical Year* had helped him to discover the liturgy; Raymond Brucker, novelist convert, whose powerful personality enlivened many a recreation at Solesmes; M. Léon Dupont, "the holy man of Tours," propagator of the devotion to the Holy Face and of the medal of St. Benedict, who came to consult Dom Guéranger about rebuilding the basilica of Saint-Martin; Henri Lasserre, first historian of the apparitions at Lourdes and friend of Veuillot, who introduced Solesmes to Charles de Freycinet and his wife, both Protestants (they said they had been won over by Dom Guéranger's charity, but forgot everything during the expulsions). And finally, there were the visits of Mérimée in 1835 and Taine in 1862.

The count de Falloux met Dom Guéranger through Madame Swetchine, whom he escorted to Solesmes on September 11, 1854. On numerous occasions, he went back to visit the abbot and in 1863 received him at his château du Bourg d'Iré in Anjou. Because of vast differences in temperament and background, the politician and the monk could not agree on fundamentals during their endless discussions on Catholic liberalism; where Dom Guéranger deplored the weakening of truth, Falloux saw nothing but nuances, dictated by circumstances. But their mutual charity and esteem never suffered from these intellectual differences.

Dom Guéranger had many other friends in Anjou, such as his old school chums: Léon Boré; Abbé Jules Morel; Charles Louvet, mayor of Saumur, who showed him the beauties of Cunault; Abbé Pasquier, pastor of Notre-Dame in Angers; M. de Quatrebarbes, who came to Solesmes to learn how to refute the Gallicans; Abbé Baugé, the eccentric pastor of Candé and discoverer of old manuscripts whom the monks nicknamed *"le père l'affût"* (Father On-The-Lookout); and finally, numerous professors of Combrée, drawn by the entrance into the monastery of their confrère, Dom Couturier.

Dom Guéranger also found friends in the region of Nantes, such as Abbé Fournier, future bishop, and his assistant, Abbé Hillereau, whom Dom Guéranger helped found the collegiate church of Saint-Donatien. Brittany first learned of Solesmes through Dom Gardereau. The Council of Rennes in 1849, in which Dom Guéranger participated, gave the Breton clergy the opportunity to show their enthusiasm for the champion of the Roman liturgy.

But Dom Guéranger didn't enter Armorica until 1855. On the road to Vannes, on the outskirts of the town of Theix, his vehicle overturned. Unharmed, he found the local church, whose patron was St. Cecilia, and he promised to bring to the parish a relic of the martyr, which he did three months later. In 1870, finances drove him all the way to Lorient, where he found the abbé Sliebusch, who had offered to help.

These friendships were the groundwork for the future abbeys of Kergonan, founded under the abbatiate of Dom Delatte.

Dom Guéranger made other friends in Marseille, and then in Artois around the college of Saint-Bertin of Saint-Omer; each led to a Solesmes foundation.

Despite his numerous friendships in France and abroad,

Dom Guéranger never forgot his native province. He loved its green countryside and the old patois (*"le vieux parler"*); he enjoyed collecting some of the expressions, which he used at times with his monks. He was proud to belong to a land with such a flourishing monastic past.

While he was still a young man, on March 24, 1835, la Société d'Agriculture, Sciences et Arts of Le Mans admitted him to membership. Although he never had the time to distinguish himself there through direct participation, anymore than at other such societies, he encouraged the works of Dom Piolin and Dom Renon, fellow members of these organizations.

Other than his trips to Le Mans, where he would stay several days to deal with his editor or his printer, he rarely took trips through le Maine except to attend a religious feast, such as the dedication of a church or the blessing of bells. He also went to La Flèche to preach the communion retreat to the youngsters of the Prytané, or to Château-du-Loir for the commemoration in 1867 of the martyrdom of Monseigneur Berneux in Korea.

Among the villages of the district of Sablé—Poillé, Fontenay, Vion, Parcé, and others—he visited Precigné most often. It had a vibrant minor seminary, whose two hundred students liked to make excursions to Solesmes, where they lunched under the linden trees of the abbey. While there, Dom Guéranger would send their brass band to give an *aubade*—a morning concert—to the marquis de Juigné. Other colleges, notably Sainte-Croix in Le Mans after 1872, made pilgrimages of the same sort.

Beginning in 1852, the abbot of Solesmes regularly visited the château de Bois-Dauphin in Precigné to converse with Mlle Paule de Rougé, who insisted on having him guide her in a spiritual journey she had undertaken. With his help, she founded at nearby la Vairie the little community of Sisters of the Holy Name of Jesus. Several days before his death, Dom Guéranger advised her of a coming visit—the last letter he ever wrote.

In 1869, the château de Sablé was purchased from Count Camille de Rougé by the duchess de Chevreuse. She immediately got in touch with Dom Guéranger, as did her two sons, the duke de Luynes, who died in combat the following year, and the duke de Chaulnes, who became a benefactor of the monastery. As for the marquis de Juigné, from the very start in 1833, he had shown a special regard for Solesmes, a care that he passed on to his son, elected deputy of la Sarthe in 1870, and to his other descendants. Among these benefactors to the abbey was the marquise de Champagné from the château de Craon, who more than once came to the aid of the abbot of Solesmes.

No one knows how many friends Dom Guéranger had in the city of Sablé. Outside of the families Cosnard and Gazeau, they were generally folk who had been drawn back to God by his spiritual presence. Conversions, far more than material interests, make for deeply rooted friendships.

Born in Sablé, but later settled in Cholet, Mocquereau (the doctor) heads the list starting in 1836. His son, the future Dom André Mocquereau, would enter Solesmes the year of Dom Guéranger's death. In 1848 Dr. Rondelou appeared; his tall silhouette became familiar to the abbey, where his generosity flowed freely for half a century. His brother-in-law, Félix Huvé, mayor of Sablé from 1858 to 1862, had a sister, Mme Félicie Bruyère, who was mother of the future abbess of Sainte-Cécile. On such occasions as a marriage and baptism, these families would invite the abbot of Solesmes, who would take the occasion to prepare a new soul for a return to the faith. This was how he met General Bourbaki, who from unbeliever became another good friend of the abbey.

Léon Landeau was among the dearest of Dom Guéranger's nearby friends. Their first meeting, in 1836, was fortuitous. One morning before daybreak, while crossing the yard of the marble factory to bathe in the river Sarthe, Dom Guéranger stumbled over the feet of a sleeping man; it was the young owner, the descendant of a family of marble manufacturers from Sablé, who had decided to spend the night at the factory. Both men were amused, and the ice was broken.

Dom Guéranger first straightened out the soul of his new friend, following which he blessed his marriage, baptized his three children, scrutinized their education, married them in their turn, and began the process all over again with the next generation. From his cell he could see his "dear children" on the roof of the *moulin*—the marble factory just down the hill. During his travels, he wrote some of his most colorful letters to them. The Landeau family was intelligent, affectionate, and trustworthy. They became so involved with the life of the monastery that they were nicknamed "the monks from just down below."

Starting in 1858, Dom Guéranger presided over the annual festival of the marble workers, which took place during the summer. The Mass was celebrated at Notre-Dame-du-Chêne, followed by lunch in the meadow of Vion. At one of these celebrations, the abbot blessed the tall fluted marble column that still stands in the square in front of the basilica. When the Saint-Clément marble factory was built opposite the abbey (on the Juigné side of the Sarthe), the marble workers' banquet was held in Solesmes. After Mass in the parish church, Dom Guéranger crossed the river in a boat to take part in the banquet prepared in the ateliers.

From time to time, Dom Guéranger's Sablé friends would

ask him to attend meetings of the Conférence Saint-Vincent-de-Paul or regional assemblies at Notre-Dame-du-Chêne. He also liked to appear at the ancient Marian sanctuary with one of his monks or some family friend. Several times, he took the entire community, notably on September 25, 1872, in union with the first pilgrimage from la Sarthe to Lourdes, in which thirty-odd inhabitants of Solesmes participated. Two days later, at eight in the evening, the monks went out to the road to meet the returning pilgrims and the entire assembly marched into the parish church singing canticles.

The abbey, which become part of the religious panorama around Le Mans, also became a stopping-point for pilgrims. When they returned from Notre-Dame-du-Chêne, they made it a habit to "stop by the monks." In response to the great movement of pilgrimages that swept France after 1870—a movement Dom Guéranger considered a sign of spiritual renewal—the parishes asked permission to enter the abbey church in procession, banner to the fore. This, among other examples, signaled how the local ill will of the first days had dissipated. Many elements converged to ameliorate local suspicion—the dedication of the first Benedictine pastor of the parish of Solesmes, Dom Follenfant; the rectitude of Léon Landeau, mayor of the community; the good grace with which "Father Guéranger" presided yearly over first communions and the distribution of prizes; the blending of the monks with the parish community on such occasions as the proclamation of the dogma of the Immaculate Conception; and, generally, the abbot's growing prestige, which redounded to the village.

When the prefect of the Sarthe asked Dom Guéranger in 1868 what effect closing the monastery by government fiat would have on the region, Dom Guéranger could respond quite truthfully that it would be disastrous. With the approach of Easter in 1870, the pastor of Sablé, Abbé Dolibeau, sent a lamb to Dom Guéranger with the inscription: "In witness to union in the Roman doctrines." This moving gesture says it all—for his countrymen, the abbot of Solesmes had become a living sign of fidelity to the Church.

X

FOUNDATIONS

THE NUMEROUS VESTIGES OF ANCIENT MONASTIC FRANCE, with their recent memories, elicited a deep yearning for its restoration by many in nineteenth-century France. To this end, friends of Dom Guéranger offered to guarantee the economic viability of a foundation or promised to furnish monastic aspirants. Many would point out that this or that former monastery was for sale, and hopefully enclose a description of the buildings. Still others simply implored him to establish a monastery at some designated spot.

As early as 1835—Solesmes was two years old at best—Cluny was being offered for 200,000 francs. Dom Guéranger also heard talk of Saint-Michel de Frigolet, which a newspaper in the south of France reported had already become a Solesmes foundation. The names of Chezal-Benoît, Montmajour, Sainte-Bertin d'Arras, and Saint-Malo came up. A pastor from la Mayenne had premature visions of Benedictines on his property at Anges, near Craon. Dom Fréchard, a former monk of Saint-Vanne, was able to persuade the abbot of Solesmes to come to Lorrain in 1844, but not to adopt his house of Vézelize. And M. Dupont of Tours was equally unsuccessful on behalf of Marmoutiers.

If the invitations came from bishops, they were of course more attractive, since they offered an easy solution to the delicate problems of jurisdiction. As early as 1838, Monseigneur Montault encouraged the founding of a monastery in Anjou on the Baumette, but he died, and Dom Guéranger turned to Monseigneur Affre—which led to the unhappy experience in Paris.

In 1844, Monseigneur Parisis offered a château near Langres as a monastery. Around 1850, negotiations were undertaken with Monseigneur Dupanloup concerning Fleury-sur-Loire, which Dom Guéranger wanted because of the relics of St. Benedict, but they ended in failure. Then, in 1856, Monseigneur Gerbet proposed Saint-Michel de Cuxa in his diocese of Perpignan. Three years later, the bishop of Autun again spoke of Cluny while, at the same time, the bishop of Fréjus made him a gift of Lérins, which Dom Guéranger refused because of its excessive isolation. Souvigny was mentioned twice by Monseigneur de Dreux-Brézé ("What beautiful churches await you"), and Monseigneur Bourret insisted that he adopt the great Romanesque nave of Conques in the heart of Overgue, a strong Catholic region.

In another manifestation of monastic fervor, Monseigneur Freppel invited Dom Guéranger to settle on the banks of the Loire, at Saint-Maur de Glanfeuil. A foundation would in fact be established there by Dom Couturier. (It emigrated in 1901 to Clervaux in Luxembourg.) On another occasion, at the request of his friends from Artois, Dom Guéranger went to examine the ruins of the Cistercian abbey of Clairmarais near Saint-Omer. The project proved unrealistic, but the relationships formed eventuated in the foundation of the two monasteries of Wisques.

Fully occupied with the mission of restoring the Benedictine order in France, Dom Guéranger did not envisage doing anything abroad. But the possibility of persecution at home persuaded him at least to consider it, always with the thought of returning when the political climate permitted. During the troubles of 1848, he instructed Dom Pitra to search out the south of England for this purpose, and, indeed, a half century later the Solesmes communities were forced to move there temporarily.

But this was not the only foreign adventure. Cardinal Pitra, for missionary or ecumenical reasons, leaned toward establishing a foundation at Saint-Anne in Jerusalem (Dom Leduc had even thought about China), but, in the end, he decided that Rome was the more ideal spot for a foundation. Rome, he reminded, had asked the Benedictines for a comprehensive renewal of liturgical books.

But the most impressive proposal came from the Holy See itself in March 1849. When the Propaganda Fide put Monseigneur Fornari in charge of finding monks in France for an apostolic mission to Norway, the nuncio contacted Solesmes. Dom Guéranger consulted his community; recalling the life of St. Anschaire, the monk-apostle of the Scandinavians, they responded with enthusiasm. The abbot drafted a memorandum outlining his conception of the monastic apostolate, but it arrived too late at Gaëte, and a plan of the Bavarian Redemptorists was chosen in its stead.

Following the debacle in Paris, a monastery in Acey in the Franche-Comté was founded which was to be villified in the pamphlets of the ex-monk Dépilliers. This monk was sent in search of financial support in eastern France and persuaded Dom Guéranger that the Franc-Comtois would provide the recruitment and income necessary for a new monastery there.

The hope was legitimate. The former monastery of Notre-Dame d'Acey with its excellently kept conventual buildings was situated in the north of the diocese of Saint-Claude. The property was acquired by Solesmes in 1852 for 60,000 francs. But Dom Guéranger imprudently made Dom Dépilliers its sole lawful proprietor. Four priests and two brothers moved in during the following spring. In the autumn, their abbot joined them. He would return twice in the next two years.

In short order, Dom Dépilliers, filled with jealousy, quarreled with the prior of the foundation and looked for his removal; since the request was, in fact, blackmail, the abbot thought it wise to recall his monks in 1856.

In the meantime, the Franc-Comtois people, at whose side the monks had devotedly remained during the cholera epidemic of 1854, had shown sympathy for the little community of monks, and Dom Dépilliers exploited them to the full. When Solesmes censured his conduct, he appealed to Rome, temporarily circumventing the Congregation of Bishops and Religious, and attempted to reinstall monks to his property. But he ended up turning his best supporters against him. Excluded from the Order in 1865, and suffering from a persecution complex, the poor man ended in apostasy. Although the entire episode saddened Dom Guéranger immeasurably, it did not shatter him—his peace of mind and natural buoyancy were too integral to his character.

At the same time as the Acey disaster, a dream of Dom Guéranger became a reality—the foundation of Saint-Martin in Ligugé—which came about through his friendship with Monseigneur Pie. When he was vicar general of the bishop of Chartres, Abbé Pie came up with a project—to revive the former monastery of Saint-Père, "in the shadow of Notre-Dame" (de Chartres). But at the time, Dom Guéranger was caught up in ending the Parisian affair and he put off the venture.

Although Monseigneur Pie did not abandon his idea when he became bishop of Poitiers, his sights shifted to the monastery he considered the most ancient of France, Saint-Martin de Ligugé, around ten kilometers south of his episcopal town. Dom Guéranger was somewhat more cautious—vocations and money were sparse—but their friendship seemed to overcome every obstacle. Monseigneur Pie underwrote a community of sixteen monks, and, as a precaution, offered the foundation as a house for auxiliary priests, a caution that somewhat disturbed the abbot of Solesmes.

On November 24, 1853, the first four monks arrived, led by Dom Guéranger. The next day, on the fourth anniversary of his episcopal ordination, Monseigneur Pie celebrated "the reestablishment of monastic life in the place where St. Hilary founded it among the Gauls, and the reestablishment of the devotion to St. Martin in the place where his holiness had most prominently burst forth." On that same day, the diocese took up the Roman liturgy once again.

From the start, the little priory led an uneventful life, greatly aided by a group of dedicated people, such as Madame du Paty de Clam and Madame Pie. But the bishop was the inspirational genius. He understood perfectly the meaning of Dom Guéranger's monastic work: to give back to France its centers of prayer, its points of spirituality, in the same places where they had shone in the past, thus signifying the continuity of Tradition. It was for this reason that he wanted the monks to use the sanctuary of St. Martin.

"I love your work as I do my own eyes," he wrote to the abbot of Solesmes, who answered, "I love this work as much for your sake as for its own sake. I know all that it has cost you." Monseigneur Pie acted as counselor and protector, with an exquisite sensitivity; he attended to material details while exercising a firm tutelage. With great charm and simplicity, he would accost railway company agents with Dom Pitra's *Spicilège*, a yet unpublished book of the Fathers of the Church, hoping to persuade them to support the monk's scientific work by granting them fare reductions.

Through his care, the church was restored and the buildings enlarged. Each year, he came to celebrate the feasts of St. Benedict and St. Martin, bringing with him some member of the episcopacy. He was concerned about the monastery, which was not as vigorous as he would have liked twelve years after its foundation. In general, Dom Guéranger did not care to become involved in direct spiritual apostolate. But he did make two monks available to the bishop to give missions in Poitou. Moreover, as at Solesmes, he favored the library and encouraged studious research, such as the works of Dom Pradié, Dom Plaine, and Dom Chamard. Ligugé was particularly dedicated to church and monastic history.

The foundation would remain a branch of Solesmes as far as recruitment went—since the constitutions of 1837 had not obtained familial autonomy—despite its conformity to the mind of St. Benedict. Dom Guéranger therefore had to form the future monks of Ligugé himself. He also went two or three times a year to handle any problems that might have arisen. This journey was a new source of joy for him: he was refreshed by a sense of repose that came from the site and the freshness of the Valley of Clain (despite the railroad line that bordered the garden), but principally from seeing his sons again. But, truth to tell, much of the time alloted to them was given to Monseigneur Pie.

When in 1864 he judged the moment ripe to endow Saint-Martin with its own abbot, he recalled a monk from Germany, Dom Léon Bastide, whom he had loaned to the young abbey of Beuron to instruct in Solesmes's way of thinking. A former imperial procurator at Villefranche-de-Lauraguais, Dom Bastide hesitated to accept the abbatiate. But his rule was a happy one; the impression given by his correspondence with Dom Guéranger is one of peace in the midst of hard work in the tiny monastery.

There was a mutual attachment between Solesmes and Ligugé; they formed one family. They forged a bond by the continued exchange of letters, the on-going invitation—practically obligation—to the monks of Saint-Martin to drop by the mother house whenever in the vicinity, and Dom Guéranger's bracing visits.

Solesmes' choice for a second foundation, Sainte-Madeleine de Marseille, is at first glance rather perplexing. Dom Guéranger had already experienced the problems that come with a distant foundation; he dreaded the journeys—in this case two days by train—that were indispensable to a young community; and he disliked the thought of installing his monks right in the middle of a large city, with all the noise that entailed. But a whole slew of circumstances converged to guide him to the choice, events in which he discerned the divine will.

The first two times he saw the place were when he was on his way to Italy in 1837 and 1843, during which times he visited the former monastery of Saint-Victor and Notre-Dame-de-la-Garde. During his third trip to Rome, in 1851-1852, he got in touch with the Catholic elite of Marseille. Abbé Timon-David, his friend, introduced him to a young man who had a vocation for Solesmes. This young lawyer, Théophile Bérengier, had a sister, Madame Durand, who was under the spiritual direction of a typical Marseillais priest, Canon Coulin, founder of a popular catechism study group. In this intricate relationship lay the seeds for a foundation.

After he became secretary to Dom Guéranger, Dom Bérengier began to dream of a monastery in the south, a dream encouraged by his friends. The abbot of Solesmes refused to "hasten the moments of Providence." But in 1863, Dom Bérengier convinced the elderly Canon Coulin, who had become a great admirer of Dom Guéranger, to turn his work over to the Benedictines.

By this time, Dom Guéranger was "better disposed to colonize Provence." But his health had deteriorated, and with it his ability to make decisions. At this point he received an invitation from the bishop of Marseille to come and participate in the festivities surrounding the consecration of the new basilica. Father abbot accepted, and during the days in June 1864 dedicated to Notre-Dame-de-la-Garde, he spoke of his hopes for a foundation to Monseigneur Cruice, and received approval for the project. Along this time, Cardinal Pitra came from Rome, overjoyed to be with his former abbot—it was to be their last time together.

France was then undergoing a wave of anticlericalism; government threats from MM. Rouland and Bonjean, secretaries of state, were upsetting the religious communities, so Monseigneur Pie counseled prudence. But Dom Guéranger's subsequent hesitation to proceed with his plans in the face of this danger caused consternation among the benefactors of the future monastery, until finally Canon Coulin flared up: "Our Marseillais subside quickly when they cease to be at the boiling point. Here, timidity is ruin!" His friends took up the pen so effectively that Dom Guéranger was forced to go through with the project.

The choice of a superior was the next difficult question. Dom Guéranger recalled Dom Menault, the former prior of Acey, from Ligugé, with all his strengths and weaknesses.

On July 11, 1865, Dom Menault arrived in Marseille. The

charter of the priory's foundation was dated July 22, feast of St. Mary Magdalen. Before the end of the year, three fathers and two brothers had joined him. Even though the monks did not enjoy the same protection they had under Monseigneur Pie, the friends they could count on were exceptional in their own way. Most astonishingly, at least from the viewpoint of Solesmes, there never seemed to be a real financial problem, thanks to the devotion of the Marseillais.

The location of the priory (rue d'Aubagne), on the other hand, left much to be desired. Although it was on the same site as the old Benedictine territory of Saint-Victor, the space was cramped and unhealthy. The stifling heat affected the health of the more delicate, even causing some premature deaths. And then there was the noise—the cries of the vendors and conversations of the passers-by penetrated the cloistered areas. These hardships became so pronounced that the monks' benefactors offered them weekends in the country. There was also talk of purchasing a country house, but Dom Guéranger thought it would be dangerous to the monastic life; he preferred transferring the monastery to the outskirts of the city. This, however, provoked enormous protest among the grand dames, and the abbot of Solesmes was forced to give in. "After all," he conceded, "as impractical as this priory on the rue d'Aubagne is, it at least has cost me nothing more than *un grand merci* [a big thank you]."

The general character and activities of the monastery were dictated by its urban setting and the contract signed with Canon Coulin. Many people expected a ministry for which the monks were not always prepared. Fortunately, they had among them Dom Lemenant des Chesnais, a former Breton missionary, who flourished in the Midi. At the request of the bishop of Marseille, he inaugurated monthly—and very successful—ecclesiastical retreats. Dom Guéranger was pleased to discover that the retreatants sang the office with the monks; he himself gave them spiritual instructions in 1869.

But when parents asked the monks to take charge of the education of their children, Dom Guéranger balked. These religious could hardly assume a full-time professorial function, when they were already hard-pressed to fulfill what they had on hand. The institution of altar boys was another question. These little ones were confided to the care of the young Dom Gauthey, a marvelous choice. Old photographs show the young boys perched on the steps of a repository altar or grouped around the future abbot of Sainte-Madeleine. Shortly before his death, Dom Guéranger allowed the very best of these children to stay at the priory as alumni. He sketched out a rule for them, analogous to the one that regulated the small oblates of the monasteries in Spain and Italy. In time, however, inconveniences arose and a damper was put on these educational activities.

The correspondence between Solesmes and Marseille is filled with bad health, the cholera epidemic, lack of personnel, troubles with the Commune of 1871, and problems in reconciling ministerial duties with the observance of the rule. On four occasions, Dom Guéranger went himself to intervene in his dear priory in the Midi, so far from the mother house. He renewed friendships and regulated thousands of details. But primarily he comforted hearts with his contagious enthusiasm. "We sang like mad [*avec un affolennement sans pareil*]," said Dom Gauthey in old French. "Father abbot sang with us—he conducted and we swept the choir along—we were very happy."

One month before his death, Dom Guéranger again went to Marseille. It was his last journey. He pondered the future of this house whose growth had been so difficult; but the monks were solidly rooted and lived the Solesmes ideal. Later, the foundation faced the hazards of exile to Italy with great courage; the monks were to return to France in 1922, where they settled at Hautecombe, in Savoie.

There was a particular reason why the priory of Marseille was so dear to Dom Guéranger's heart. "Without Saint Mary Magdalen," he would say, "I would never have founded Sainte-Cécile."

In founding Ligugé, Dom Guéranger had responded to the wishes of Monseigneur Pie; in founding Marseille, he had listened to a group of friends. In both, he began to realize the program contained in the constitutions of 1837—building the Congregation of France. Founding a monastery of nuns, however, was something new and unplanned, although manifestly the will of God. Dom Guéranger's confidence in that will was affirmed in 1868 when he said: "I have done this work so as not to disobey God."

Saint-Pierre was born because Guéranger wanted it. The vocations followed. For Sainte-Cécile, the vocations came first—living signs that he should found it. The first vocation, the future head of the new work, was someone whom he had prepared for the role a very long time without realizing it.

The Bruyère family was introduced to Dom Guéranger by Félix Huvé around 1850. When in 1853 the Bruyère family acquired the manor of Coudreuse, on the commune of Chantenay, three leagues from Sablé, they began to visit the abbey frequently. M. Léopard Bruyère, a retired architect, had lost his faith. His eldest daughter, Jenny, was born in Paris on October 12, 1845 (the day on which Solesmes celebrates the anniversary of the consecration of its church), at a time when Dom Guéranger was undergoing great trials.

The first meeting between the prestigious Benedictine and the little eleven-year-old girl became a favorite memory.

Returning from a walk to Solesmes, Dom Guéranger met Madame Bruyère, who introduced her child, whom the abbot had agreed to prepare for her first communion. The monk bent over her, smiling, and said, "We're going to get along very well, aren't we, my child?" *"Oui, mon père."* The response was timid. It would take years of patience before Dom Guéranger could win over the one he called his "little mute."

Dom Guéranger immediately began to form this young soul. Whether on a visit to Coudreuse, or through letters to Paris where the Bruyère family passed the academic year, he made sure that the young girl (already well grounded by her mother) received constant spiritual direction, never thinking of a future religious life for her. Without impinging on her secular duties, he taught her the simple rules of his own spirituality—perfect submission to the will of God by breaking down one's will. "When you are supple, open, sympathetic, obliging, ready to please, and finally rid of the concentration that stems more from stiffness than from peaceful contemplation, then Our Lord will be your master."

Since he was dealing with a soul of good will, gifted with great intelligence, his counsels bore fruit. Instead of retreating into sullen piety, this strong-willed and highly tempered girl evolved into a smiling and generous person. The abbess of Stanbrook would later write: "Wisdom and simplicity seemed to play in and all about her, strength and softness, activity and unalterable peace, extraordinary intuition, and childlike grace." Her solemn character and doctrinal bent continued to rule her, but they were balanced by the human qualities of the heart.

Cécile—she had chosen the name upon her confirmation in Chantenay in 1858. Even as a child, she had wanted to give herself to God, a secret she did not immediately confide to her spiritual father. On October 12, 1861, after the Mass of

Dedication and at the end of a year of secret "novitiate," she pronounced a private vow of chastity before Dom Guéranger, who gave her a ring. Shortly thereafter, she admitted to him she wanted to live the cloistered life, the only form she knew; this came as no surprise, since he had suspected it for years.

Her avowal nevertheless troubled Dom Guéranger; the spirituality of the convents of the time, which had been influenced by the eighteenth century, was hardly satisfactory, but he had no intention of becoming involved in a fight for reform. When Madame Bruyère suggested (she was the first) that there be a Solesmes for women, the abbot protested: "I have never thought of such a project. I know all too well by experience the enormous work, the care and difficulties, that a foundation brings. I have spent my life launching one, and I haven't the years and strength to set my hand to this new work."

But the idea gnawed at him; it even broke into his prayers. He tried in vain to thrust it aside, but ended by confiding in his confessor, Dom Couturier. This good man responded: "Rather than new worries, Father, isn't it a consolation to know that the Lord is preparing the last years of your life in this way?"

But Dom Guéranger did not want consolation; he wanted to do the will of God. And little by little he perceived signs of it until, around 1863, he confessed he had become "converted" to the concept. From then on, he openly instructed Cécile in the Benedictine spirituality.

Although the project, still vague, was fraught with difficulties, Dom Guéranger knew that he could count on the help of the new bishop of Le Mans, Monseigneur Fillion, one of his most faithful friends. The bishop, moreover, was heartily in favor of an establishment of Benedictine nuns close to the abbey, of having in his diocese a second house dedicated to the life of the Church, as prescribed by Dom Guéranger.

As though they were signs of approval, other vocations began to surface. Two young ladies from the environs of Sablé, Henriette Bouly and Honorine Foubert, who were acquainted with Cécile Bruyère also aspired to the Benedictine life.

A nest of vocations, moreover, was discovered by Dom Guéranger on a journey to Marseille in 1864; it came from the "seminary" of Canon Coulin. The abbot proceeded slowly, prudently, at first speaking only of the dignity and nobility of religious life. Two years later, he unveiled to some of them his tentative plans for a new foundation in Solesmes. It was then that the solidity of the formation provided by M. Coulin became apparent, as well as the efficacity of the presence of D. Merault in Marseille, and above all the spiritual magnetism of the abbot of Solesmes.

Dom Guéranger's last doubts were dissipated, and he pressed forward. But at this point the situation changed dramatically. When M. Bruyère became aware of Cécil's religious vocation—which, among other matters, nullified his matrimonial plans for her—he became enraged and threatened to do all in his power to close Saint-Pierre de Solesmes. Since the minister of Justice and Worship had already shown what he was capable of, Cécile begged Dom Guéranger to launch the foundation without her. But he refused, for in his mind she had been chosen to head the new community. In consequence, they proceeded very quietly with their project until the very last moment.

In Marseille, the announcement of the entry of the first postulant nun into Solesmes caused a passing storm in some families who thought they had been hit by a veritable Benedictine epidemic. But Dom Guéranger calmed their fears. On two occasions during 1866, hope foundered—insufficient funds. Near the end of the summer, however, construction finally began on the downslope of a hill in the middle of the fields in Solesmes.

Dom Guéranger had given up his original idea of installing the founding nuns in a provisional structure. Rather than wait for the end of the construction, he decided to house them, along with several lay sisters from the area, in a house in the village which would be called *"Sainte-Cécile la petite"*(Little St. Cecilia's).

On November 16, the feast of St. Gertrude, monastic life began, humbly, but under the direction of a master. Sainte-Cécile was not to suffer the uncertainties and jolts of the first years of Saint-Pierre. Dom Guéranger felt a resurgence of youth: for the first time ever, he said, he was not disappointed.

Many elements joined in contributing to the harmony of the new convent, not the least being the master of novices. Father abbot once more took up this role, initiating the postulants in the celebration of the office and regulating the observance of the Rule. With Dom Guéranger, even recreations were instructive: he would be seen crossing the street from Saint-Pierre on his way to Sainte-Cécile, carrying books on Bosio or Rossi, to instruct his new postulants on the marvels of subterranean Rome.

Cécile Bruyère, the designated superior, seemed to have no fault other than her youth, which worried some of Dom Guéranger's friends. "It's a shortcoming," he would answer wryly, "which I don't find upsetting, inasmuch as it's the only one I'm sure is corrected daily." Back in 1833, he had had the same "shortcoming."

The tiny community showed qualities, such as obedience, that would have been instructive to the first Solesmians. Their youthfulness may have helped. But their diverse temperaments were cause for worry. Dom Guéranger secretly

wondered if such a house—half Marseillaise, half Sarthois—
might not explode. But, in fact, the dynamism and efferves-
cence of the former balanced the slightly cold heaviness of the
latter. "Marseille and our region have united," he noted
gladly. "The fusion is such that in the house one can make out
neither North nor South." He himself was attracted by the
warmth and open character of the southerners.

The vocations were numerous and solid. Princess
Catherine de Hohenzollern, protectress of the new Abbey of
Beuron, was among the first to ask to be admitted. But Dom
Guéranger turned down this slightly imposing postulant,
believing she would be more useful to the Benedictines in
Germany.

On the financial end, despite good management, the
picture was dim, the resources so bad that the poverty at times
became sheer destitution. The appearance of the new buildings, with their bell-turrets and neo-Gothic embellishments,
was misleading. In truth, Dom Guéranger more than once
was forced to borrow in order to continue Sainte-Cécile.

The monastery was no more than a construction site
when, to everyone's surprise, Dom Guéranger decided to
transfer the foundresses there on August 14, 1867, to give
them the habit. It was in character that, once having decided
on the worthiness and feasibility of a task, he should go at it
with vigor.

Sainte-Cécile's memorable dates proliferated:

—August 15, 1868: the first professions, for which Dom
Guéranger composed a new ceremonial. By joining the rite of
profession with the consecration of virgins (then in disuse), he
underlined the specific character of feminine contemplative
monasticism in the great family of St. Benedict. The day after
her vows, Mother Cécilia was elected prioress, and Dom
Guéranger charged her to take effective direction of her house.

—July 14, 1871: benediction of the first abbess, twenty-six years of age. Unbeknownst to Dom Guéranger, the favor of allowing for such a young abbess had been asked of Pius IX by Monseigneur Fillion during an audience on July 14, 1870. The date was supremely fitting—the first abbot of Solesmes had been chosen by the Pope on July 14, 1837. Although unaware of this, Pius IX had remarked to the bishop that it was like putting "the cart before the horse," since the monastery had not yet been raised to an abbey. But, he admitted, the cart was already rolling along quite well. Besides, he wanted to show his gratitude to the author of *The Pontifical Monarchy*. If this could not be called precisely a dream come true for Dom Guéranger, it did cement his belief that the plan had been destined by Providence.

—October 12, 1871: dedication of the church. Dom Guéranger had followed its construction very closely. Its main purpose was, of course, to offer divine praise. When he heard his daughters sing the divine office with an inimitable fervor, he was filled with joy: "Less than ten years ago, there was wheat growing there!" He wondered if this marvel might not be traced to the prayer of some unknown Solesmesian monk of old.

Like their brothers at Saint-Pierre, the nuns received daily instruction from their father, but with greater enthusiasm, judging from their notes. His studies contained—along with matters pertaining particularly to the vocation of nuns—all his most cherished ideas: enthusiasm for the Divine Office, along with the wish to acquire a deeper theological under-standing of it, using such material as the *Summa* of St. Thomas; attachment to the Church and concern for its great causes; constant orientation of the heart and mind to Christ, contemplated as bridegroom; zeal for the salvation of souls; and, finally, a joy and gaiety, perfectly compatible with dignity—"to be alleluia from head to toe," as he loved to put it.

Mère Cécile Bruyère knew how to make this doctrine live; it was said that she became the faithful mirror of it. She did, in fact, quite often repeat Dom Guéranger's exact words, or at least the general sense of his thought; she reviewed all of his correspondence and his writings to help prepare the materials for his first biography. But she ranged farther: like any true disciple, she had so assimilated the teachings that she in turn became a spiritual master.

The contemplative life appeared to her to be the celebration of the unique liturgy of heaven, which brings the soul to a life of infinite Beauty and Truth. Thus she fashioned a theology of contemplation, which Dom Delatte would discover and develop further. In 1885, the abbess published *The Spiritual Life and Prayer, According to Holy Scripture and Monastic Tradition*, a treatise in which she dealt with her spiritual message nourished by experience of the things of God, experience which Dom Guéranger had instigated in her.

At first, little was said about the foundation of Sainte-Cécile, which was later to exert such a profound influence. "These works make themselves known by their fruits," wrote Dom Guéranger to Monseigneur Pie, as if to excuse the lack of publicity. To his friends, he showed a deep satisfaction in the work through revealing comments, as: "This little garden that I plant to the glory of God in my old age. . . ." Or, on another occasion, referring to the bishop of Poitiers, "He pretends that I am one of those fathers who has a last child in his old age, and who is more tender with him or her than the others, above all when it's a girl."

The establishment of a convent of young nuns in proximity to a monastery of men carried psychological risks, as much for the monks as for the town population. On top of which there was the well-being of the superior, already over-worked by the steady influx of monks, and now stretched further by his having to take charge of a community of women as well. But Dom Guéranger managed things with so fine a touch that though he personally assisted the nuns when need arose, especially in the beginning, his monks were never jealous. In truth, they were also affected by the beauty and importance of the work.

Understanding the distinct vocation of each, the abbot of Saint-Pierre never treated his sons and daughters identically, except in his devotion. If nothing else, it reflected his own aversion to uniformity. In the end, the relationship between the two monasteries was healthy, balancing between them their qualities of strength and refinement.

Summing up the causes of his gladness, Dom Guéranger in 1868 wrote these words: "Our Lord is known, loved, and served truly faithfully in this little sanctuary. It is a challenge, in our times, to the Revolution, yet the first Christians were bolder still."

XI

KNOWING HOW
TO INHERIT

BY THE TIME THE FIRST VATICAN COUNCIL OPENED, the abbot of Solesmes had almost become a patriarch of nineteenth-century monks. He had been one of the first to instigate monastic renewal, not only in the physical sense—rebuilding the ruins left in the wake of the revolutionary tide—but also in his attempts to recover the early, simple spirit of St. Benedict. The movement to return to the sources through the study of Tradition was bearing fruit in religious life as well as in ecclesiastical scholarship.

The experiment pursued at Solesmes inevitably attracted the attention of foreign Benedictines who, less shaken than the French by the fall of the *Ancien Régime*, felt, if somewhat confusedly, the need of a general reform, if not a total renewal. On returning to his monastery after a stay in Solesmes, an Austrian monk wrote as much to Dom Guéranger: "It is a different life from ours, a life animated by the spirit of another century. It's true. The spirit of the holy Rule, the great strength of the liturgy, the splendor of the divine office, the plainsong, is exactly what we lack—consequently, the essential things."

This and other such responses confirmed for Dom Guéranger that his work had not been in vain, that he had helped others discover how to bring about a Benedictine renaissance.

The way in which the spirit of Solesmes spread through Germany seemed to him to be more in line with the proper character of monasticism than what was being pursued in other countries. Although Dom Guéranger never himself crossed the Rhine, he received the founders of Beuron at his house, counseled them, and loaned them one of his monks to help them get on their feet. This mode of renewal—propagating a way of thinking, mutual monastic aid, and a respect for national diversities—appeared preferable to legal affiliation. Similarly, Sainte-Cécile de Solesmes's influence spread rapidly to Jouarre, Sainte-Croix de Poitiers, and Stanbrook.

But however many the demonstrations of esteem for him and his work, Dom Guéranger remained deeply humble. One day he overheard Dom Bérengier, his secretary, compare Solesmes with Cluny in front of some visiting monks. He brought his secretary up short: "You are only thinking about playing a role, about cultivating an image! A monk must think of God and how to serve the Church!"

This leads to a thorough review of Dom Guéranger's conception of monasticism. The preceding pages have dealt with Dom Guéranger's vision of the relationship of the monastery with the Church, of his conception of its liturgical role, its labors, and its internal organization. The following pages will deal with his views on the Benedictine tradition and his work in restoring monastic life.

He was often urged to write about his thoughts on these questions, and as he grew older, his monks and friends pressed him to publish the *Life of Saint Benedict* which he had promised to do for a long time. They hoped in this way to have a clear definition of the meaning of the Benedictine institution.

Although the work never progressed beyond manuscript form, it is absorbing. Dated 1869, it reflects thirty years of monastic life. As Dom Couturier said in 1878, "Dom Guéranger was not born all in one piece; he himself liked to recall that not only books, but experience made him go forward every day in what constitutes the essence of monastic life."

Other sources are also revealing, notably several letters during 1832-1833 which spoke of his feelings and intuitions, such as those concerning the *Rule for the Novitiate*, which principally oversees the spiritual formation of the young. There were also exchanges in the late 1860s with Dom Maur Wolter apropos of a Benedictine confederation.

Moreover, according to those close to him, Dom Guéranger knew how to harmonize teaching with living— that is, his lifestyle gave evidence of the principles he proclaimed.

To evaluate the importance of Benedictine monasticism, Dom Guéranger placed himself in a historic perspective. He began with a general assertion: "The Order of St. Benedict is the great fact of Western Christianity, because its influences have acted, through the centuries, upon religious and political society, and because the diverse religious families which have succeeded one another for eight centuries stem from it, come from it, or are founded on its traditions."

He then reviewed the sources of St. Benedict's thought. Benedict, he knew, inherited the monastic experience of the East, which itself had roots in evangelical times:

"The Benedictine institution did not rise up on its own in

the Church. It was, rather, an intelligent product of Eastern monasticism. Monasticism was a form of Christianity as old as the Church herself. It was born in the East, as was our faith. It is in the East that the terrestrial angels [Saint Paul the hermit and the other Fathers of monasticism] appeared with the mission to implant this sublime life and to carry it in one single stroke to its highest expression."

Dom Guéranger reaches back even farther, to the era of preparation: "In order to put St. Benedict and his work in the correct light, one must go back to the time of Christianity that preceded it and, as it were, to the origin of all things; for while it took many centuries to extend over the whole world, monasticism flourished early here on earth; the seeds, it could be said, were scattered about from the very beginning of the world."

Basing his thoughts on the writings of the Church Fathers, he cites all the "monastic" figures of the Old Testament who prefigured Christ, the true models of monks. "What, then, is monasticism," he concludes, "this grand thing which the ancient world bore within itself and which, if we believe the Fathers, seems to have harvested the excellent fruit of Christianity? *It is the state in which man, raised from the original fall by Jesus Christ, works to reestablish himself in the image of God by virtually separating himself from all that can cause sin.*"

This search for evangelic perfection makes the monk a sign of the work of salvation: "God has done nothing greater than the mystery of the Incarnation, of which the Church is but an extension. Now, the Church has a heart: the religious state. This is the most complete manifestation possible here below of the mystery of the Incarnation—an exact reproduction of the life of Christ."

Returning to the life of St. Benedict, Dom Guéranger considers it archetypical of monasticism. Like the first monks of the East, Benedict began by hiding in order to live only with God, with no thought of influencing his time. But God transformed him and made him into a light for the world:

"The spirit of his Rule being an effective separation from the world, Benedict had already expressed this reality fully merely by his manner of living. But because he had become like unto Christ in the tomb, the hour of the Resurrection had also to arrive for him, so that he, too, might appear as a type of resurrected life which his disciples must profess in serving the Church and the souls of the faithful.

"First, a hermit deep in a grotto; later, as abbot of twelve monasteries, he saw the apostolate stretch before him. This, then, was the destiny of Western monasticism, of which he was called to become the legislator and model.

"First the desert, the hidden and crucified life of the cloister; later the apostolic ministry in the middle of heathen nations, the works of sanctification and of Christian civilization in the midst of barbarous peoples, who were just then coming into contact with Christianity. Finally, we see Benedict whole, and in him the complete idea of his mission."

This mission was fully understood by popes and bishops: "To create a civilized Europe, they had an element at hand which never failed them and which helped them accomplish their entire work, the monastic element."

Here again is the theme so abundantly treated in the nineteenth century; but Dom Guéranger emphasizes the spiritual outreach of the monks of the Middle Ages rather than their manual and literary work.

St. Benedict saw himself as the inheritor of the monastic tradition, and his successors were expected to imitate him. From the myriad aspects of the work he undertook, one valuable lesson stands out, and Dom Guéranger drew several conclusions from it.

First, he insisted on the primacy of charity, of union with God—that is, of contemplation—the secret of apostolic radiance: "Prepared by God himself, full of God, united to God, the monk will be productive, with a productivity that cannot be compared to that of others. This love of brethren, of the Church, that inspires his prayers, his work, his penance in the cloister, will overflow into human society, and history will judge the degree of life which the Church attains in any given century in proportion to the esteem rendered the religious state, the number of its representatives, and what they do."

As noted, Dom Guéranger uses the terms "monastic life" and "religious life" interchangeably. In his eyes, monastic life was "the principal and most complete form of religious life," or, better yet, monastic life was religious life in its original state, unmodified, the Christian life led with an aim to perfection. Benedictine monasticism, unlike other religious families, is not oriented towards a particular goal.

In the development of religious orders over the centuries, monasticism was like a vigorous trunk, whose sap gave birth to a multitude of evangelical branches. The process continues to this day; it will never cease to produce new forms adapted to the various eras. But in every age, side by side with its new manifestations, it will continue to exist in its pure state, as an example and a force kept in reserve by the Church.

The contemplative school of St. Benedict will always be indispensable in preparing men for whatever mission is needed by the Church. Yet the monk is not a man who can do any work at all; rather, he is a man entrusted with praising the divine, a man of the Church, adhering to the universal principle of all vocations. To this the order of St. Benedict owes its exceptional and ongoing life.

As early as 1832, Abbé Guéranger had challenged the common perception that a monk is bound to erudite studies.

"Throughout the centuries," he wrote Abbé Gerbet, "the cloister prepared men of vast genius in Europe—original, and above all, suitable for the contemporary society." But little by little, some specialization appeared, which Dom Guéranger regretted. "The time of absolutism," he went on, "which was the age of regular clerics, restrained the monastic spirit, but it did not destroy it, and it reappeared, forthright, hardy, full of vigor and independence, ready for anything, as in the days of Alcuin, Hildebrand, and Bernard. It was only in the era when they could do nothing other than be scholars that monks concentrated all their energies on collating manuscripts."

Even making allowances for the idealization of the Middle Ages, one nevertheless senses, as Dom Delatte put it, "an exact idea of what Benedictine life ought to be." Dom Guéranger's letter to Abbé Foisset was in the same vein. Written shortly after July 11, 1833, he applies the fruit of his reflections on Benedictine history to the works he has just begun:

"I am in no way a partisan of congregations who surge up with a plan that has been completed in advance; in it, the ideas of man predominate. We are experimentally searching for the will of God in the direction which you see—study of Catholic tradition, history, then later biblical exegesis, excluding neither philosophy, nor poetry, nor even the natural sciences.

"Monks praying and studying, ready for all that God might want of them; as you must know, that is the reason for the continuance of the Benedictines for over twelve centuries, the reason they have never become tied to any particular type of specialized activity but have been able to render service in all areas—thanks to the blessed freedom of the Spirit of God."

Dom Guéranger did not refer to the monastery's liturgical functions, since his correspondent had inquired about the work of the monks. But it seems quite possible that the monastic experience gave him an even clearer awareness of the primacy of the Divine Office. Still, the essential in this letter was the insistence on a monk's readiness to serve, guided by the Holy Spirit.

In short, Dom Guéranger did not intend for his monks to become agriculturalists, or academicians, or missionaries, or professors. Although he didn't consider any of these occupations incompatible with monastic life—assuming these activities were conducted in line with the essentials of cloistered life—he refused to give them any official status. But he did understand that the good of the Church, or that of the monastery, sometimes required exceptions, demanding that a monk for a time, or forever, leave his cloister, as witness Dom Pitra, the perfect example, or Dom Leduc, tapped by the Holy Spirit to found an apostolic work. "The monk outside his monastery," he would say, "is like a fish out of water." But if he leaves through obedience, "he will not lose the merit of contemplation in active life, for his roots remain in solitude, to which he willingly returns, just as he would always have remained there had he not been pushed by the Holy Spirit to leave it."

These special cases aside, Dom Guéranger refused to engage his community in activities that risked losing it its monastic identity. When, for example, he asked his monks to take on a missionary activity in the Scandinavian countries, he took great care to specify the conditions under which this apostolate would be undertaken. After all, it was in the interests of the Church to safeguard the cloistered life.

By nature, Dom Guéranger was opposed to reducing everything to a system; he believed that, except for the immutable monastic principles, the Benedictine cannot be constricted by a definite program. His constitutions of 1837 give proof of this.

The prologue to these constitutions enumerated which points the monks of Solesmes should concentrate on to attain the goal of serving the Church, such as support of the Roman doctrines, a deeper study of Tradition, and so on. When he learned, in 1864, that Dom Maurus Wolter proposed to insert this text into the constitutions of Beuron, Dom Guéranger explained to him how it ought to be interpreted:

"It is obvious that this prologue is completely French, and 1837 French at that. After stating the intention of reestablishing the essential practice of the Rule of St. Benedict, it goes on to attack Gallicanism, which is of primary importance to us. In Germany, there are different requirements. The writing needs to be completely reworded. One could, for example, insist on helping to reestablish the traditions of the Catholic Church in respect to the celebrations of the Divine Office, the exercise of the sacred liturgy, and the administration of the sacraments; as well as reestablishing and maintaining the spirit of faith in the people who have been exposed to the breath of the rationalism of these times. . . . The nuance is not the same for the two countries. We were established with a militant goal, and if it is given to me to bring all things to completion, modifications will then certainly be required by changing events."

When he stated that "the monastic life is a life of traditions," the abbot of Solesmes carefully weighed each of his words. He had meditated a great deal on the example of St. Benedict, on his sense of balance, and on his wisdom in adapting monasticism to the Western world, and had come to appreciate in its fullness his well-informed sense of tradition.

This understanding of the monastic spirit, characterized as it was by freedom, without which there is no life and consequently no tradition, explains Dom Guéranger's aversion to centralization. He was led to air his thoughts on this significant problem on the eve of the First Vatican Council. Dom Maurus Wolter, who wished to reaffirm the cause of the Benedictines, asked Dom Guéranger to help him put a confederation on its feet, and to define the essential elements of monastic life. In response, the monks of Solesmes jotted down the remarks of their abbot:

"That which makes the Jesuits strong," Dom Guéranger said, "will be a danger to us. Each monastic family takes its physiognomy from the country in which it is established. Fervent and flowering abbeys evolve of themselves; the others do not reform themselves simply through the exercise of authority. A monastery, a living thing, a being of tradition, renews itself by doctrine, prayer, and the devoted efforts of a few, by generously imitating a neighboring example of fervor, and by returning to its beginnings and the conditions of its birth.

"This has been our history for over fourteen centuries. The day we are centralized will be the day when reform will become impossible, spontaneity having been abolished, replaced as it were by very perfect administrative cogs which will imitate life, but which are not life."

Dom Guéranger appears here as a renovator, carefully rediscovering the seed of life sown by the great founders which, little by little, had been buried under excessive organization—the almost inevitable result of human activity. Nevertheless, out of friendship for Dom Wolter, who came to see him in 1869, he agreed to define the bases for what he called a "fraternal union" of monasteries—the term itself sought to shed any sense of administration but to connote federation, confederation. In the name of the general character of monasticism, he insisted that the familial autonomy of St. Benedict be respected:

"The Order of St. Benedict, in its essence, is not an active militia, but a school of contemplative life; and the monks who vow to search for their own individual perfection in the silence of the cloister, in the celebration of the Divine Office, in work, obedience, mortification, and stability have no need of centralized organization, which is necessary for the active reserves of the Church, so that their members can be employed in the diverse tasks to which they are vowed by their vocation. Those who have entered into these orders look for action to procure the glory of God; the monk chooses the laborious repose of the cloister so as to live with God."

As a man of tradition, Dom Guéranger was committed to searching out the original truth in the thinking of the Fathers. He was aware that he was only a humble link in this living tradition, which he was careful never to break or entangle. He knew how to pick up the monastic experience, not unthinkingly, or imitatively, but in order to make it flourish in his own century. The fact that the Congregation of Solesmes had been declared the inheritor of the ancient French Benedictine Congregations in 1837 did not require it to copy Cluny or Saint Maur. Yet many of their principles were adopted, such as in organization. Moreover, far from renouncing the freedom that characterized the old days, Dom Guéranger proposed to apply the evangelical principle, *nova et vetera* (things new and old), which he found throughout the Benedictine Rule. It penetrates deeply into the meaning of his best-known maxim: "It is by St. Benedict's Rule that we shall be Benedictines."

Monasticism appeared to him to be so closely tied to the Church, to the Gospel, as to share their perpetual youth. "The Church is immortal," he wrote in his 1846 *Historical Essay on the Abbey of Solesmes,* "and the monastic institution, which is an integral part of the Church, continually renews itself with her." The return to the source was essential for this rejuvenation.

Dom Guéranger was not a man to waste time on conjectures about the future or nostalgic regrets about the past: he was content with the present. But, of course, from time to time, he did look back to reflect on his experiences and to profit from them.

Although he did not document his forty years of monastic life, much can be drawn from a variety of other material. The overall impression is of laborious progress. After the joyful preparation, after the enthusiasm and hopes at the beginning, the reality arrived with all its sharpness: battles outside and inside the monastery, the threat of ruin and scandal, and much else besides. But fortified by the word of Rome, Solesmes held fast, until finally, thanks to the lessons of experience, his dedicated friends, and his own perseverance to a great cause, the monastery took root.

Without seeking any such title, Dom Guéranger had become "the erudite abbot of Solesmes," the principal authority on liturgical matters. He had seen liturgical unity triumph in Rome, and, in his last controversy, he had helped the fathers of the Council to stop hesitating by shedding light on the doctrinal foundations of the dogmatic definition of papal infallibility, which frightened many—principally the Gallicans in France.

To his contemporaries he reintroduced the meaning of the Church's prayer, which nourished contemplation. By word and example, he showed that the Church was not a venerable and aged institution, but a living entity. By reestablishing Solesmes, he tried to give back to the Church in France her centers of ecclesiastical life, to bring about once more what the monks in the past had done for her.

In his monastery, he was a father, around whom his sons gathered; around these sons, in turn, the extended family of guests and friends assembled. His generosity of heart was so great that no one came to him in vain, no matter how disparate the range of requests; his assistance, of course, was more moral than material.

Dom Guéranger was the resolute enemy of routine, tepidity, and naturalism; he spent his energies communicating his faith and his enthusiasm. Of this trait, Cardinal Pitra remarked in 1875: "We who have lived, prayed, and meditated with him, will miss above all the apostle of the supernatural order, the man of faith who had such a marvelous insight into the meaning and tone of things divine."

But beyond the simple optimism, or his "enormous groundwork of cheerfulness," as he liked to put it, he radiated supernatural joy—a condition of holiness—as prescribed by St. Benedict.

At age twenty-three he exclaimed: "Happy are they whose life or death contributes to the victory of truth, because the Truth is God!" An abrupt dictum, uncompromising, like its author. But far from forging this truth in his own image, he always sought it from Tradition, that is to say from the Church, to whom God had confided it. Dom Guéranger's friends were well aware of this. "As for you," said Etienne Cartier one day, "I love you not only as a father, but as the representative of the Church and of truth, upon which my intelligence and my will can build in complete confidence."

Of this ardent and disputatious monk, God had made an artisan of peace, for there is no real peace outside of the truth. He had achieved it in the freedom of spirit achieved by the humble, who are able to perceive the action of the Holy Spirit through events. Dom Guéranger's wisdom, moreover, allowed him to understand and deal with realities.

His life, however, was never free of gropings and false steps, deceptions and sufferings. The growth in the number of monks was long in coming, and at times the quality of the vocations left something to be desired. And his foundations progressed slowly; Dom Guéranger was never able to attain the three abbeys needed for a meeting of a General Chapter, which he wanted in order to deal with some grave problems. Nor had Solesmes found its economic balance: father abbot carried the weight of its debts to his death; in fact, the day after his death, a liability of 500,000 francs was discovered. Finally, to the great regret of his friends and readers, he left his principal works unfinished, and nothing at the time indicated that his sons would have the talent or energy to complete them.

"The whole of Dom Guéranger's existence," observed Mme Cécile Bruyère, "was limited by God on nearly all grounds. When he tried violently to break open the bonds, failure, as in Paris in 1845, recalled him rudely to reality."

Difficulties and incompletion—the two words encompass what the first abbot of Solesmes came up against. And if he ever held any illusions, his friends would immediately dispell them. "Your enterprise is a masterpiece," wrote M. Desgenettes to him as early as 1833. "The one who was your inspiration for it will make you pay for the workmanship."

A few years later, Madame Swetchine wrote these lines, intending to comfort him: "I have never doubted that you would have to put up with many setbacks: the task is in proportion to the energy of him who endures it. But you have within you the energy, the power which destines a man to some special work. You were born a Benedictine, or rather the abbot of Solesmes. You will also walk in the footsteps of the most holy founders, and when you make a mistake from time to time, it is the qualities which constitute your spirit and your character that will overcome all and achieve your goal."

It would be interesting to know how Dom Guéranger judged these psychological considerations at the end of his life. Gifted by rare energy, there was still nothing of the superman about him and he kept constant guard against the tendency to be domineering. He seems above all to have drawn his strength from his simple submission to the will of God.

His vision of things was enlightened by his perception of the Incarnation and the Redemption as the center and law of history: God builds his work by founding it on the sacrifice of Christ and utilizing imperfect workers. Instead of insisting on an ideal situation, instead of outlining a perfect program only to complain when reality steps in, Dom Guéranger shouldered his cross daily as prescribed by God. "Circumstances make the saints, saints do not make the circumstances," he loved to say. His friends admired the patience he displayed with reverses and sufferings. But another aspect of his endurance escaped them, an aspect that could only be perceived by a soul that has experienced the relative monotony of cloistered life: "Often," writes Mme Cécile Bruyère, "in thinking about our father abbot, Dom Guéranger, it seemed to me that certain martyrs would view these long years passed among so many temporal and spiritual worries with admiration; [he never] seemed to look for distraction nor for an existence outside the monastery to compensate for the troubles on the inside. This daily perseverance was a beautiful fidelity *in multa patientia* [with great patience] a generosity that did not feed on the sublimity of acts, but on obscurity and a continuous life of abnegation." (Cf. Mt. 16.24)

As for imperfections and the incompletion of his work, Dom Guéranger was the first to convict himself. He was not blind and knew that certain people imputed this or that deficiency at Solesmes to the abbot. As he himself said:

"I tried to give my monks the most exact monastic doctrine, but I had no illusion: I lacked the men; the resources too. I will never be surprised that others can do better. I could do no more than make a beginning, lacking means, and I do not believe Our Lord will reproach me for it. I am but a poor man, whose insufficiencies He knows well."

Nor did he want "reform" to be spoken of:

"One reforms what is decadent after it has attained its perfection" he explained. ". . . I believe I have done practically all that is possible out of the elements that were given to me; I couldn't do any better. I aim towards amelioration year by year. If Our Lord gives me more useful elements later on, all the better; but I can honestly say to myself that if Solesmes is not perfection, never at least has it made one step backwards. If therefore in the future everything falls into place and starts working, that will not be reform, but the completion of foundation."

"The mission of every man is limited," he wrote in 1864 after the death of Father Faber, and perhaps thinking of himself. He often expressed the wish that his sons take his place. This hope concerned all aspects of the work of Solesmes. Monseigneur Pie reminded the monks of the responsibility they would assume as inheritors of their abbot:

"If Dom Guéranger's mission was not to complete everything that he began, it is evident that he was charged by God to begin many things that his children would bring to completion according to the traditions that he left them. I am quite confident about what will happen at Solesmes in one hundred years. There is here a projection of intelligent holiness which is part of the father and will most certainly spread forward. There is in this neither vanity to conceive nor humility to affect; all of it comes from God and from the father that he gave you."

The heritage would be put first in the hands of the next abbot of Solesmes; but to follow a strong personality is difficult indeed. Dom Guéranger was all but certain that after his death his mantle would go to his prior, Dom Charles Couturier, whom all agreed was the perfect disciple. By temperament, the two men differed in many ways. Reserved, a little timid and careful, and with almost a sad air, Dom Couturier had a horror of the least controversy. But his doctrinal firmness could lead him to acts of heroism, as was seen during the expulsions of 1880. Still more than his wisdom, his goodness attracted hearts, and his coat of arms— a beehive with the motto: *Consortia tecta* (sheltered communities)—symbolized his attachment to the familial character of the monastery and the congregation.

Did Dom Guéranger feel totally understood by Dom Couturier? A delicate question and clouded in speculation. But shortly before his death, the abbot had the presentiment that Cécile Bruyère, his spiritual daughter from whom he kept no secrets, would have a particular function to assume. "He did not think to act against prudence," writes Dom Delatte, who depended on the abbesses's own notes, "in confiding a mandate of prayer to the inheritor of his thinking and his monastic principles, a mission of example, and a benevolence for the whole family of which he was the leader."

At the beginning of October 1874, Dom Guéranger received, along with other guests, the man who in 1890 would become his second successor, the future Dom Paul Delatte. To this twenty-six-year-old assistant pastor of Notre-Dame de Roubaix, the peace of monastic life seemed ideal for his intellectual studies. The tall priest must have towered over the aged patriarch of Solesmes as he listened to the abbot speak of the true goal of Benedictine life. But Abbé Delatte felt ill at ease and decided not to return. Dom Guéranger regretted his inability to persuade a man to enter in whom he found the qualities of Dom Pitra, and perhaps something more. But his benediction of the priest bore fruit: seven years later, the abbé Delatte gave himself to the monastery.

By formation as by temperament, Dom Guéranger and Dom Delatte resembled one another hardly at all. The former understood doctrine principally through historic evolution, whereas the latter, formed in Thomistic philosophy, attained it in a more speculative manner. But although they lived in different times and resolved different problems, their monastic thinking united them. Both lived "as if they saw the invisible," and Monseigneur Pie's testimony to Dom Guéranger applies equally to Dom Delatte: "He was a true contemplative. He had what every Benedictine must have: a constant and exclusive preoccupation with God."

Men gifted with strong vitality cannot become accustomed to the idea of an impotent old age. Dom Guéranger wished to die while still active; his desire was granted.

His correspondence attests to his ongoing bad health. If he was spared intense suffering, he never really knew what it was to be well. He held on, above all, through sheer will power. He had stomach pains every morning, dating back to his seminary days. His exposure to cholera in Rome in 1837 also left traces—Dom Guéranger remained sensitive to the heat which, he said, took ideas away from him. The best remedy consisted in a dry, cold winter, which le Maine did not provide.

But finally, his fatigue, accentuated by prolonged vigils and his refusal to take a vacation, brought on in 1864 an anemia that lasted for over a year. His journeys, moreover, taxed the enfeebled body more and more and walking became painful. But since he hid his illness under a persistent cheerfulness, everyone at the abbey finally stopped worrying about him.

Dom Guéranger's discretion about his mortifications was

even more successful. Not until after his death were hair-shirts and disciplines (small whips) with little chains discovered; before there had only been speculation.

The peace of his last years was not from inaction. His last work, *Saint Cecilia and Roman Society,* cost him such effort that it probably contributed to his end.

In December 1874, his condition improved and he visited his foundation in Marseille once more. On returning, he was so exhausted that he left his cell in the priory and moved into the ground floor of the abbatiale. Angina prohibited any big effort, but it was difficult to keep Dom Guéranger still. Although he never spoke of a wish to leave this world, in keeping with the spirituality that he had always taught, he held himself ready for anything that God willed.

Those who witnessed his last days recalled numerous details so well that the unfolding events could be followed hour by hour. From the whole there springs an impression of a peaceful and serene end. And, right to the end, Dom Guéranger the father could not leave without saying adieu. On the evening of January 27, the brother who called him at the usual time for a conference at Sainte-Cécile saw he was exhausted and tried to dissuade him from going out. "No," said the abbot after a brief hesitation, "I want to go. Poor children! This is perhaps the last time they will see me."

The next day, at midday, after having received several visits, he took to his bed. Doctor Rondelou held out no hope: the man was worn out. Dom Guéranger fell into a painless doze, broken by moments of delirium during which he murmured psalm verses and scraps of liturgical formulas. He would repeat the "*Spiritu, in Spiritu*" beginning of the Offertory prayer, which he loved, as well as "*Credo. . . credo. . .* Men so diminish faith!"

In between, he was quite lucid. On Friday the 29th, he

received Extreme Unction; then began the prayers for the dying. At his request, his favorite psalm was recited, *Benedic anima mea Domino* (Psalm 102, Bless the Lord O My Soul), then the *Te Deum*. His room was accessible to all—monks and friends. From time to time, the dying man would greet this or that person with a smile. Dom Bastide returned from Ligugé and Dom Leduc from Angers. The nuns, constantly appraised of the situation, organized a vigil of prayer. Dom Guéranger learned of it and appeared to derive comfort from it. "My daughters are praying for me," he said to Dom Couturier in the course of the night. Perhaps he recalled having told the abbess how much he feared a difficult agony, to which Mère Cécile had replied that she would obtain from God an exemption of it for him.

The agony was in fact quite mild. Reunited around their father abbot, who smiled at them with open eyes—his unforgettable blue eyes—the monks gave him a farewell kiss. The abbot of Ligugé begged him to remember them all before God. At 3:30 in the afternoon, Saturday, January 30, 1875, Dom Guéranger delivered his soul to God.

The religious took turns near the deceased reciting the psalter, as is the monastic custom. Wednesday, February 3, he lay in state in the north transept of the church, in the chapel called Notre-Dame-la-Belle which he had loved. Near 4:00 in the afternoon, as the bells of the two abbeys resounded, he was carried in procession to Sainte-Cécile to the singing of the *In paradisum*. Vespers of the dead was sung by the two choirs, then the monks brought the coffin close to the grille, and the nuns, after Compline and Matins, passed the night in prayer. In the nave, the men of the parish took up the guard of the deceased, some workers keeping vigil until morning.

Dom Guéranger had won the hearts of the people of the region; the newspaper reporters at the burial were struck by it. The presence of the bishop of Le Mans, the prefect of la Sarthe, and the town administrators of Solesmes and Sablé was to be expected, given the stature of the deceased. But what stunned was to see so many of the common folk arrive from Sablé and the surrounding countryside to salute "Father Guéranger" for the last time.

One month later, on March 4, 1875, Monseigneur Pie gave the funeral oration. The bishop of Poitiers spoke of many things, but mainly of the accomplishments of his friend. This discourse was complemented a year later by one given by Monseigneur Freppel at the anniversary service. The bishop of Angers examined the principle that drove Dom Guéranger; he showed how this man, before all, had been a monk, a man of divine praise, a man of God, and as such, a man of the church, and therefore a man of the Roman Catholic Church.

The Church herself, through Pius IX, immediately recognized the services rendered by the deceased abbot: the Brief *Ecclesiasticis viris*, dated March 19, 1875, began by praising the zeal and scholarship of Dom Guéranger, and pointed out three ways in which his works had exercised a determining influence on the minds of his time: the definition of the dogma of the Immaculate Conception, the definition of the dogma of papal infallibility, and above all the return of the dioceses of France to the Roman liturgy.

Somewhat surprisingly, the document did not mention the reestablishment of Benedictine life in France, Dom Guéranger's principal accomplishment. But as if reading the public speeches of Monseigneurs Pie and Freppel reminded him of this omission, Pius IX was quick to recover. In the Briefs of greeting which he addressed to the two prelates, the Pope affirmed that Dom Guéranger's greatest gift to the Church and to the Chair of Peter had been his monastic vocation and his role as the abbot of Solesmes. This summed up the entire life of this man who had wanted only to be a monk "living more for God and for his neighbor than for himself."

Dom Guéranger's body lies today in the crypt of the church of Saint-Pierre de Solesmes. His heart was placed at the foot of the altar in the abbey of Sainte-Cécile: such had been the wish of the father.

For these two monasteries and their numerous foundations, for their friends, and for all Christians, Dom Guéranger lives on as the sign of a life given entirely and loyally to God and to his Church. If he merited being recognized by Pius IX as a "true son of St. Benedict," it was probably because of what he did for the monastic order, and for having affirmed, by word and deed, the actuality of St. Benedict's mission, whose spirit continues to attract strong vocations to the service of the Church.

But perhaps it was primarily for having constantly sought to instill in his monks, nuns, and contemporaries the knowledge of what the Church principally is—a society of divine praise.

That sums up Solesmes, which accords with the wishes of St. Benedict. No one has put it better than Monseigneur Freppel: "To praise God and to cause God to be praised—all Dom Guéranger's work is in this single thought. The rest is but a consequence and a development. There is the true meaning of his mission and the unity of his life."